Special Plays for Holidays

SPECIAL PLAYS
for HOLIDAYS

by
HELEN LOUISE MILLER

Publishers   PLAYS, INC.   Boston

Library of Congress Cataloging-in-Publication Data

Gotwalt, Helen Louise Miller
Special plays for holidays

Summary: A collection of fifteen one-act plays celebrating holidays throughout the school year, from Halloween to Mother's Day.
1. Holidays—Juvenile drama. 2. Children's plays, American. 3. One-act plays, American. [1. Holidays—Drama. 2. Plays] I. Title.
PS3513.075S64 1986   812'.52   86-9332
ISBN 0-8238-0275-2 (pbk.)

Manufactured in the United States of America

Contents

The Greedy Goblin

Characters

MR. STRUDEL, *baker*
MR. WHITMAN, *city detective*
MRS. WHITMAN, *his wife*
JASPER WHITMAN, *their son*
JOE
JERRY
KAREN } *students*
BETSY
GOBLIN

TIME: *The night before Halloween.*

SETTING: *Whitman living room. Small stand is center. There are at least four chairs, a telephone, a table with black thread in the drawer, and a desk with paper on it and four flashlights in a drawer. Exits are right and left.*

AT RISE: MR. WHITMAN *and* MR. STRUDEL *stand, center.* JASPER *sits, reading newspaper.*

MR. STRUDEL: I'm telling you, Mr. Whitman, this is the last straw! I cannot stand any more! I baked five hundred pieces today, and how many do you think were stolen?

MR. WHITMAN: Well, Charlie, if you can tell me how many of those pies were pumpkin custard, I'll tell you how many were stolen.

MR. STRUDEL: I baked four hundred and fifty pumpkin custards on special order for Halloween!

MR. WHITMAN: Then four hundred and fifty pies were stolen! No pumpkin pie is ever safe in this whole town!

MR. STRUDEL: Then why doesn't someone catch the gang that is stealing the pies? Are you a detective or a village blacksmith?

MR. WHITMAN: We're doing all we can. You go on back to your bakery. We're bound to break this case in another twelve hours. *(Phone rings;* MRS. WHITMAN *enters, answers it.)*

MRS. WHITMAN *(Into phone):* Yes, he's here. . . . Oh, that's too bad! . . . Yes, I'll tell him right away. *(Hangs up)* Mr. Strudel, that was your wife. She wants you to come home right away. The new batch of pumpkin pies disappeared off the cooling racks.

MR. STRUDEL *(Shrieking in despair):* I can't stand it! The new batch, already stolen from the racks! Some detective you are! *(Exits)*

MRS. WHITMAN: This is really terrible, John. Can't you do anything about it?

MR. WHITMAN: We're knocking ourselves out at headquarters. If we don't catch this gang of hoodlums before tomorrow, the police force will be the laughing stock of the town.

JASPER: Don't you have any clues at all, Dad?

MR. WHITMAN: No more than what you see in the paper. Those reporters know as much as we do.

JASPER: "The Greedy Goblin Strikes Again"—that's the headline in tonight's paper, Dad.

MR. WHITMAN *(Sarcastically):* Very clever! That headline came from the notes that were left at the scene of some of the pie thefts.

JASPER: But can't you get fingerprints off the notes, Dad?

MR. WHITMAN: There aren't any fingerprints. Just the name—"The Goblin"—written in greenish ink that the crime lab can't seem to analyze.

JASPER: That's funny! No fingerprints!

MR. WHITMAN: None. And Mr. Strudel isn't the only victim. There's not a section of the town that hasn't been touched. Stores, church basements, schools, bakeries, private homes—any place that has a pumpkin pie has been hit.

JASPER: We're having a meeting here tonight, Dad, to replan our school Halloween party. If we can't count on pumpkin pies, I guess we'll have to switch over to cider and doughnuts. But, what's a Halloween party without pumpkin pies?

MR. WHITMAN (Grimly): Things are tough all over, son. But don't worry. We'll get those thugs, if it takes every man on our force. (Begins to put on coat and hat) Don't worry if I'm a bit late, Mary. We're going to put everything we've got into this case tonight.

JASPER: You know, Dad, I've got a theory on this thing. . . .

MR. WHITMAN (Sighing): Sorry, Jasper, I've got no time for theories tonight. What we need is action. So long. (Exits)

JASPER: I wish he'd waited to hear my idea.

MRS. WHITMAN: He's too busy and too worried, Jasper. The whole pumpkin pie business makes him look and feel awfully silly. Now, tell me how many people are coming to your committee meeting.

JASPER: Just four. Jerry, Joe, Karen, and Betsy. Why?

MRS. WHITMAN *(Smiling):* Oh, nothing . . . I might just have a little surprise for you. . . .

JASPER: What's the big secret, Mom?

MRS. WHITMAN: I know these committee meetings make you boys and girls terribly hungry, and so I just thought I'd try . . . *(Looking around nervously)* I almost hate to say this . . . but just before supper I baked a . . . you know what . . .

JASPER: Mom, you had the nerve to bake a . . .

MRS. WHITMAN: Sh! Not so loud! Yes, I did.

JASPER: But where is it?

MRS. WHITMAN: It's next to the refrigerator—at least it was a few minutes ago.

JASPER *(Jumping up):* For Pete's sake! Don't leave it unguarded for a single second! I'll go look and see if it's still there. *(Exits)*

MRS. WHITMAN *(Calling after him):* Don't cut into it while it's still warm. *(Doorbell rings.* MRS. WHITMAN *opens the door.* JERRY *and* JOE *enter.)* Hello, Joe. How are you, Jerry?

JOE: Hello, Mrs. Whitman.

JERRY: Fine, thank you. Is Jasper here?

MRS. WHITMAN: He'll be back in a minute. He had some urgent business in the kitchen. *(Calling)* Jasper! Your friends are here. *(JASPER enters.)*

JASPER: It's still there, Mom, but you'd better go stand guard. *(She exits.)* Hiya, fellows. Any news about the Greedy Goblin?

JOE: Not a thing.

JERRY: I guess we'll have to change the Halloween party refreshments. *(Doorbell rings.)* That's probably the girls. *(Opens door.* BETSY *and* KAREN *enter.)*

JASPER: Hi! The boys are here already, so we can get

started right away. *(Boys and girls exchange greetings.)*

KAREN: Did your Dad hear any more about the pumpkin pie stealing, Jasper?

JASPER: That's all he hears about from morning to night.

BETSY: But are there any more clues? I've always thought your dad was a very clever detective.

JASPER *(Defensively):* He's *still* a very clever detective, but this case is weird!

KAREN: My dad says he thinks it's funny the whole police force and detective bureau can't round up a gang of boys.

JOE: What makes you so sure it's *boys?*

JERRY: And how do you know there's a gang involved? The notes are just signed *The Greedy Goblin.*

BETSY: But it would have to be more than one person. Look how many pies have been stolen, from all parts of town, and at all hours of the day and night. *One* boy couldn't possibly cover all that territory.

JOE: There you go again—"boy!" Why couldn't it be a girl?

JASPER: Look! Are we here to make plans for the party or solve the mystery of the Greedy Goblin?

BETSY: I wish we could do both.

KAREN: Betsy and I have lined up ten dozen doughnuts and all the cider we can drink.

JERRY: I think we should hold out for pumpkin pies. Strudel's Bakery is working an extra shift. Maybe we can get some pies after all.

JASPER: Not a chance! Mrs. Strudel just called my dad before he left and told him that the new batch of pies had already been stolen off the cooling racks.

JOE *(Disgustedly):* Some police force! Sorry, Jasper, I

keep forgetting your dad is on the force.

JASPER *(Upset)*: Well, you'd better try hard to remember. I'm sick of people making cracks about the police force and the detective bureau.

KAREN: There must be *some* clues. The police just don't seem smart enough to see them.

JASPER: That's because they don't really understand the case.

JOE: Now who's criticizing the police force?

JASPER: I'm not criticizing them. I'm just saying they don't understand the case.

JERRY *(Sarcastically)*: And I suppose *you* do!

JASPER *(Firmly)*: I *think* I do. At least, I have a theory. It's really very simple. You see, there are no fingerprints. The thefts take place in widely separated parts of town at almost the same time.

JOE: So what? What's the answer?

JASPER: Don't you see? It isn't natural.

KAREN: But what's your theory?

JASPER *(Slowly)*: If it isn't natural, it must be supernatural—something that's beyond or above the natural.

JOE: Stop talking in riddles. What do you mean?

JASPER: Well, in plain English, I think the Greedy Goblin is exactly who he says he is . . . a greedy goblin.

BETSY: I still don't understand.

JASPER: I think the Greedy Goblin is a real *goblin*, not a *person* at all. He doesn't leave fingerprints because he *can't* leave fingerprints. He writes in some sort of magic ink that even the chemists can't analyze. He covers more ground and travels faster than would be possible for a human being.

JERRY *(In disgust)*: Ah, you're crazy! There is no such thing as a goblin.

JASPER: There is too. I looked it up in the dictionary and it says that a goblin is a mischievous elf or sprite.

JOE: But there's no such thing as an elf or a sprite.

KAREN: If it's in the dictionary, it's real.

BETSY: Maybe Jasper is right. But how could you prove it?

JOE *(Laughing):* It's like the old recipe for rabbit stew, first catch your rabbit.

KAREN: We could set a goblin trap!

JOE: Say, there's an idea!

JERRY: What would we use for bait?

JASPER: Hold everything, kids! Are you really game to catch the goblin?

ALL *(Ad lib):* Sure. Of course. But how? *(Etc.)*

JASPER: I have the perfect bait. Wait here for two minutes. *(Exits)*

BETSY: What's the perfect bait for a goblin?

KAREN: I feel sort of scared!

JERRY *(Feigning nonchalance):* Aw, come on, Karen— you always panic in a crisis. (JASPER *enters, carrying pumpkin pie and serving knife.)*

JASPER: Here's the bait—a fresh baked pumpkin pie!

JERRY *(Sniffing):* Mm-mm! That smells good!

JOE: Too good for any goblin!

BETSY: Where did you get it, Jasper?

JASPER: Mom made it for us to eat tonight.

JERRY: I can hardly wait to have a piece.

JASPER: Oh, no. It's not for us any longer. It's for the goblin. Bait—remember? Betsy, see if you can find a spool of black silk thread in the table drawer. Joe, you and Jerry look in the desk, and see how many flashlights there are. *(Children follow directions.* JASPER *places pie on small table center, then arranges four chairs around it.)*

BETSY: Here's the thread, Jasper. *(Hands spool to him)*

JASPER: Great, Betsy. Now, you and Karen wind the thread from one chair to the other as if you were making a thread fence. *(They start to do so.)* Did you find the flashlights, Joe?

JOE *(Holding up flashlights):* There are four here, and I have one of my own, so that's one apiece.

JASPER: Good.

BETSY: We've wound the thread from chair to chair. How does it look?

JASPER *(Inspecting thread):* That looks just right. This should make the perfect booby trap for old Mr. Goblin. *(*JOE *and* JERRY *distribute flashlights.)* Now, we're set. Everybody hide behind a piece of furniture. Keep perfectly still until you hear a crash, then focus your flashlights directly on the pie—or goblin trap.

JERRY: We're ready. I'll turn out the lights. *(Children take cover.* JASPER *flips switch. Lights go out.* JASPER *squats down behind a chair. There is a short silence.* GOBLIN *enters, takes pie, knocks over chair, and falls on floor.)*

JOE: We've got him! We've got him! *(At the sound of the crash, children turn on flashlights, revealing upset chair and* GOBLIN, *clutching pie, lying flat on his back.)*

JERRY: Quick, Jasper, turn on the lights! *(*JASPER *flips switch; lights go on.)*

JASPER *(Approaching* GOBLIN*):* So there you are! Caught at last!

JERRY *(Advancing with flashlight raised above his head):* On your feet, thief. *(*GOBLIN *jumps to feet.)*

JOE: And give me that pie. *(Takes pie and sets it on table)*

JASPER *(To* GOBLIN*):* Well, why don't you say something? You've got an awful lot of explaining to do.

GOBLIN: To you?

KAREN: To us—and to the police department.

BETSY: Jasper, you'd better phone your dad.

GOBLIN: Who is his dad?

JOE: A detective on the police force.

KAREN: He'll arrest you, of course. *(GOBLIN laughs heartily.)*

JASPER *(Angrily):* Don't laugh at my father, you greedy goblin, you!

GOBLIN: I'm not laughing at your father. I'm laughing at you. Do you actually think your father will come and arrest me and take me to police headquarters?

JASPER: He sure will. Just wait till I phone him.

GOBLIN *(Calmly):* Go ahead and call him. I'll wait.

JOE *(Puzzled):* What makes you so sure you won't be arrested? You're guilty, aren't you?

GOBLIN: Guilty of what?

JERRY: Of stealing all the pumpkin pies in the city.

GOBLIN: Oh, sure, sure. I stole all the pies, all right.

KAREN: You don't even sound sorry. You've committed a crime!

BETSY: Why did you do it?

GOBLIN: Curiosity. Every Halloween I hear you human beings raving about pumpkin pie, so I made up my mind I wanted to taste one.

JOE: One! But you've stolen thousands! Surely you can't eat all of them.

GOBLIN: Of course not. I'm saving them all for tomorrow night when I intend to throw the biggest party in Goblin Land! *(Sighs)* Now what are you going to do with me?

JASPER: We told you. We're calling my dad so he can come arrest you and lock you up.

GOBLIN *(Laughing):* Don't make me laugh.

JASPER *(Annoyed):* What's so funny, Mr. Goblin?

GOBLIN: You are! Don't you know that grown-ups can't see goblins? If you call your father and he comes tearing out here, he won't be able to see a thing. In fact, he'll be wild at you for bringing him out here for nothing.

KAREN *(Uneasily):* You mean no grown-ups can see you at all?

GOBLIN: How do you think I managed to steal all those pies without being seen? I was very careful to take those pies when there were no children around. Grown-ups don't believe in goblins so they can never see them.

JASPER *(Defiantly):* Just the same, I'm calling Dad.

GOBLIN: O.K. If you get into trouble, don't blame me. *(*MRS. WHITMAN *enters, carrying a tray of paper plates, napkins, forks, and a cinnamon shaker.)*

MRS. WHITMAN: Jasper, you forgot the paper plates for the pie. *(Abruptly)* Why are you all standing around with flashlights? Are you playing some kind of game?

JASPER: Mom, don't you see anything strange in the room?

MRS. WHITMAN *(Looking around):* Strange? Well, no. Nothing except the strange way you are all acting.

JASPER: But, Mom, we caught the goblin!

MRS. WHITMAN: Caught the goblin, have you? Well, that's fine. *(Shaking her head)* I suppose you've made up a game about it. Here are your plates and napkins. I hope you all enjoy eating the pie, and if I were you, I'd stop playing silly goblin games, and eat the pie, before somebody steals it from right under your noses. *(Exits)*

GOBLIN: You see! What did I tell you?

KAREN *(Nervously):* She looked right at you!

GOBLIN: And never saw me. That's just what your father and the policemen will do, Jasper. And you'll catch it if you call your father home for nothing.

JERRY: Maybe he's right, Jasper.

JASPER *(Upset):* But what are we going to do with him? If the rest of the goblins get to like pumpkin pie, we'll *never* have any.

KAREN *(To* GOBLIN*):* Don't you realize how wicked it is to steal?

GOBLIN: It's wicked for you to steal because you're children and you're supposed to be good. I'm a goblin. I'm supposed to be bad. I have to live up to my reputation, and besides, I want all my goblin friends to taste this pumpkin pie concoction! I know they'll like it.

JOE: If they like it as much as you do, it will be just too bad for us.

GOBLIN: To be quite honest, I haven't tasted any myself yet.

JERRY: You mean you've stolen all those pies, and you haven't tasted a single one?

GOBLIN: Of course not. That wouldn't be polite—not until I can share it with the other goblins. *(Sniffing)* But it certainly smells delicious.

JASPER: That gives me an idea. Let's have him taste this one.

JOE: Are you crazy? Then we won't even have any for ourselves.

JASPER: It's a chance. Maybe he won't like it. Maybe he'll hate it. It's worth trying. Betsy, would you cut the pie, and then we'll give him a piece.

GOBLIN: I must say this is very generous of you.

BETSY *(Cutting pie and putting piece on a paper plate):* I'll just give him a small piece as a sample. There! That should be big enough. *(Hands pie to* GOBLIN, *who picks up fork)*

KAREN: Oh, wait! Wait! *(Picks up cinnamon shaker and shakes it on* GOBLIN's *piece.)* We almost forgot the cinnamon. *(*GOBLIN *begins shrieking, throws piece of pie on floor and runs around frantically.)*

GOBLIN: Get that away from me! Don't come near me with that cinnamon shaker!

JERRY *(Puzzled):* What's the matter?

KAREN: But all pumpkin pies have cinnamon. Mrs. Whitman must have forgotten to put it in when she made it.

BETSY: So she gave us the shaker so we could put it on top.

GOBLIN *(Breathlessly):* But cinnamon is poison to goblins! It dries up our blood! Our hair falls out! What you call cinnamon is deadly goblin dust!

JASPER: Then you and your friends have had a narrow escape. There would have been a mass murder in Goblin Land if all of you had eaten those pies.

GOBLIN: Let me out of here! Let me go!

JERRY *(Putting up his hand):* Not so fast! We're not finished with you yet. Betsy, give me that shaker, please.

GOBLIN: No! No! Help! Help!

JOE: Now, we have him at our mercy! Here's our chance to get rid of him once and for all. There won't be a trace of him. Sprinkle him well, Jerry.

GOBLIN: No! No! Save me! Help!

JOE: Now's your chance to get a confession, Jasper.

JASPER *(Sternly; to* GOBLIN*):* Why did you leave all those notes at the scene of the crime, Mr. Goblin?

GOBLIN: Because I didn't want anyone else to be blamed for what I did. Not even a goblin would be that mean.

JASPER: Very nice of you, I must say. Now what did you use for ink? Our crime lab has not been able to analyze it.

GOBLIN: Firefly juice. I doubt if the chemical formula is known.

JASPER: Do you have any of it with you?

GOBLIN: Sure, I always carry a goose feather that is well soaked with it. *(Pulls feather out of pocket)*

JASPER: Then write what I dictate. Jerry, you hold the cinnamon shaker over his head. Betsy, you find a piece of paper in the desk. *(*BETSY *finds paper in desk, hands it to* GOBLIN.*)* Now, go ahead, and write as I dictate.

GOBLIN: All right. I'm ready.

JASPER: I hearby confess to all the robberies of all the pumpkin pies, which I solemnly promise . . .

GOBLIN *(As he writes):* How do you spell solemnly?

KAREN: S-O-L-E-M-N-L-Y.

GOBLIN *(Writing):* . . . which I solemnly promise—

JASPER: To restore to their owners before daybreak.

JERRY: Do you know how to keep a promise, Mr. Goblin?

GOBLIN: Yes, yes. I promise. I wouldn't want a grain of cinnamon near me.

JASPER: Keep on writing. *(Dictates)* And I furthermore solemnly promise . . .

GOBLIN *(As he writes):* And I furthermore solemnly promise . . .

JASPER: That I will never again steal another pumpkin pie from any human being, so help me Beelzebub!

GOBLIN: There! It's finished!

JASPER: Now sign it. The Greedy Goblin!

GOBLIN *(Signing):* It's signed. Now will you let me go?

JASPER: Will you promise to make copies of this confession and leave one with every batch of pies you return?

GOBLIN: Yes, yes. I promise. Now, please let me go!

JASPER: O.K., Jerry. You can put down the cinnamon shaker.

GOBLIN: And one more favor, if you please.

JASPER: Make it snappy.

GOBLIN: Will you please turn out the lights so I can make a proper exit?

JASPER: O.K. Get moving. I'll keep them off until I count to ten. *(Turns off lights and counts to ten slowly.* GOBLIN *exits, with pie. Stage lights up.)*

KAREN: He's gone!

JASPER: And good riddance!

JOE: And now, how about that pie, Jasper? I'm starved!

JASPER: Good idea!

BETSY: I'll cut us each a piece. *(They turn toward table where pie has been, only to find it has disappeared. There is a note on table.)* Why, it's gone!

JERRY: That dirty, double-crossing goblin! I should have given him the works with that cinnamon!

KAREN: Look, there's a note. Read it, Jasper.

JASPER *(Reading):* "Dear Friends: This was my only chance to taste a pumpkin pie that I knew was free from cinnamon! Believe me, I'll never take a chance on another. Please forgive me! Signed . . . The Greedy Goblin."

JOE: Of all the nerve!

JERRY: The poor guy sure worked hard to get a taste of pumpkin pie. *(All laugh. Curtain)*

THE END

The Softhearted Ghost

Characters

EGBERT ⎫
FATHER ⎬ *the Ghost family*
MOTHER ⎭
GYPSY
M.C.
BILL TEMPLETON
SILAS P. STATIC
PIERRETTE ⎫
GIRLS ⎬ *Halloween masqueraders*
TWO STAGE HANDS

Scene 1

TIME: *Halloween.*

SETTING: *The living room of the Ghost family.*

AT RISE: FATHER, *dressed in a long white robe with chain belt, is pacing floor.* MOTHER *is sitting, trying to read a magazine.*

MOTHER *(Looking up; annoyed):* I do wish you would sit down, dear, and try to control yourself. Here, read this firsthand account of a goblin raid in *The Saturday Evening Ghost.*

FATHER *(Continuing to pace):* I'll read it later. *(Worriedly)* I can't do a thing till Egbert comes home.

MOTHER: Don't worry, dear. He'll be along any minute.

FATHER: He'd better! And if that young whippersnapper has nothing to report from *this* trip, I'm through with him. I won't have a weakling for a son and be the laughing stock of the graveyard.

MOTHER: Oh, Henry, don't be so hard on him. After all, he hasn't had much experience in these things.

FATHER: Not much experience! Of course he hasn't. He's had none whatever. He won't take advantage of any opportunity that comes his way. Why, when I was his age, I had already frightened the Countess de Verne into a spasm, *and* terrorized an entire village.

MOTHER: I know, dear. You always seemed to have a natural gift for horrible things.

FATHER *(Fondly):* And what about you? Didn't you panic an entire neighborhood when you disguised yourself as the headless witch and the phantom lady? You have amazing talents, my dear, and *(Turning)*, that's why I can't understand why Egbert is such a complete flop as a ghost.

MOTHER: It's just that he's so tender-hearted, he can't bear to see anyone frightened.

FATHER *(Sighing):* I know. But no self-respecting ghost or goblin would ever admit to being softhearted. *(Discouraged)* And I've taught that boy every trick I know.

MOTHER *(Confidently):* Oh, Egbert will have great talent and ability once he finds himself, but you'll just have to give him a little more time.

FATHER: Time! He's had all the time in the world!

MOTHER: Now, dear, except for this one weakness, he's never given us a moment's trouble. Why are you so determined that he must frighten people?

FATHER: Because that's the whole point of being a ghost. Tonight is Halloween, the time of year when mortals are most susceptible to "Ghosties and ghoulies and things that go bump in the night." If Egbert can't cause at least one case of hysteria tonight, I won't allow him to participate in any of the Ghost family's celebrations ever again!

MOTHER *(Pleading):* If only you'd let me go with him. Maybe I could give him confidence. I could wear my skeleton costume with the clanking chain necklace and bracelet, and loom up behind him at the critical moment. That way, he wouldn't lose his nerve so quickly.

FATHER: Nothing doing! Egbert must do this on his own. *(Looking up)* Ah, I hear him coming. *(Assumes a commanding position with crossed arms as EGBERT enters)*

MOTHER: Good evening, dear.

EGBERT: Hello, Mother. Hello, Father.

FATHER *(Sternly):* Hello, son. How's the weather? Horrible, I hope.

EGBERT: It's a wonderful night, Dad. The wind is howling in the trees and it's pitch dark. No sign of a moon.

FATHER: Wonderful! It should be a spooky Halloween. Did you meet any people on the way home?

EGBERT: There were a few children down by the Old Mill.

FATHER: Children, eh? Out by themselves at this time of night? And by the Old Mill, too *(Rubbing his hands together gleefully)*—they would be easily frightened, especially tonight! Did you scare them out of a year's growth?

EGBERT: Well, no, er—that is . . . not exactly. You see, they were just little children.

FATHER *(Stiffening):* They scare most easily.

EGBERT: But that's just it, Dad. I couldn't bear to frighten them. In fact, I had to make myself invisible until they had gone safely by me.

MOTHER: Didn't you even give them a few moans and groans just to startle them a bit?

EGBERT: Oh, no. Children are terrified of moans and groans. They wouldn't have slept a wink all night.

FATHER (Sternly): What difference would it make if they didn't sleep the rest of their natural lives? Might have made you famous. (Sighs heavily) Letting those children escape unspooked was bad, but surely you met someone else on your walk.

EGBERT: Oh, yes, there was a young girl standing at the crossroads . . . where the old prison used to be.

FATHER (Enthusiastically): What amazing good luck that she was near the old prison. That's where the gallows used to stand. It would have been a simple matter for you to have appeared to her as the ghost of a headless horseman! Did you think of that?

EGBERT: Well, as a matter of fact, I did think of it, Dad . . . but she was a young girl, sort of timid, and she was all alone . . . so . . . well . . . It just didn't seem quite fair.

FATHER: What? Fair! What does being fair have to do with being a good ghost? I'm telling you here and now, Egbert. I've had it! You are a disgrace to the ghosting profession!

MOTHER: Oh, Egbert. Can't you tell us of a single solitary soul you have scared or startled or frightened?

EGBERT (Sadly): I'm afraid not. I guess I just don't have the right stuff in me. The minute I get all set to scare someone, I just freeze up and lose my nerve.

FATHER (Angrily): A coward, that's what you are! A lily-livered coward.

MOTHER: Henry! How can you say that about your own son?

FATHER: Easily. Egbert, you come from a long line of successful ghosts, spirits, phantoms, and zombies. You have a family heritage that is unrivaled in the spirit's world. You alone have failed to live up to it. My mind's made up. *(Resigned)* I can no longer let you live in my house, Egbert. Please pack your bags tonight.

MOTHER *(Pleading):* Oh, Henry! Please . . . for my sake . . . give him one more chance.

EGBERT: It's no use, Mother. I can see his mind is made up.

FATHER: Egbert, out of my sight, before I really lose my temper and turn you into a Japanese beetle.

EGBERT: But wait, Father! Surely you'll give me to the stroke of midnight to see what I can do. The streets will be filled with Halloween merrymakers. *(Pleading)* Will you give me a few more hours?

FATHER *(Discouraged):* Why should I? You've had years and years and you've never done the slightest thing to justify our faith in you.

MOTHER: Oh, Henry, give him one more chance. Maybe his luck will change. Perhaps he could give someone a teeny weeny scare.

FATHER *(Firmly):* I won't settle for a teeny weeny scare. Nothing less than a faint or hysterics will satisfy me. *(To* EGBERT)Well, Egbert, I'll give you one last chance. You have until midnight!

EGBERT: Thanks, Dad! You're the best father a ghost ever had!

MOTHER: Remember, Egbert, if all else fails, you can always cause a good scare with a few moans . . . work up to a crescendo and wind up with a demoniacal shriek.

EGBERT: I'll try, Mother.

FATHER: If I were you, I'd scout around till I found a Halloween party with lots of young people, and then I'd really do my stuff.

EGBERT: I'll do my best, Dad.

FATHER: I'm sure you will, my boy.

MOTHER: And good luck to you. (EGBERT *exits.)*

FATHER: Come, dear. We'll make ourselves invisible and follow him. We'll see for ourselves what he does.

MOTHER: Oh, please, Henry, won't you let me help him the least bit?

FATHER: Absolutely not! He's on his own. Come, we must hurry. *(Curtain)*

*   *   *   *   *

SCENE 2

SETTING: *Sheridan High School Gym. Piano and bench are at left. Folding chair is center.*

AT RISE: *Halloween party is in progress.* GIRLS *and* PIERRETTE, *dressed as masqueraders, are seated in a circle around* GYPSY, *who sits on chair. She is reading palms.*

1ST GIRL *(Holding up palm):* Read mine, Gypsy! I want to know if I'm going to be a banker or a model.

GYPSY *(Reading palm):* Neither one. You are going to stay at home, tend your garden, parrot, and three cats.

1ST GIRL: I don't believe a word of it. I think you are a horrible fortune teller.

GYPSY: In that case, I'll tell no more fortunes. *(Rising)* And, besides, the mystic hour of midnight is approaching. Time for us to go on a spook hunt.

2ND GIRL: A spook hunt?

GIRLS *(Ad lib):* Oh, no! Not me! I'm afraid! *(Etc.)*

GYPSY: Come on, all of you. Line up. I'll lead the way. *(They line up behind* GYPSY.*)* Piano player, get set up and give us a melancholy tune. *("The Funeral March" begins; a record can be used.)* Hold tight to the hand of the person in front of you. If any long arms reach out to grab you in the dark, you'll be safe. *(*GIRLS *shriek.)* Remember, no matter what happens, don't let go of hands. *(As music plays,* GIRLS *march slowly out behind* GYPSY. *The last one in line,* PIERRETTE, *drops out and lingers behind. She wears black and white clown suit.)*

PIERRETTE: I told Bill I'd wait right here for him. It's nearly midnight now. I wonder what could have happened to him. If he doesn't show up, I'm through with him for good. *(*EGBERT *enters.* PIERRETTE *has her back to him, and he draws himself up to full height, arms raised as if to grab her, but as he approaches, she opens her vanity case to powder her nose, and sees him in her mirror. Turning)* Oh no, you don't, smarty! What do you think you're doing, trying to scare me, just because you're dressed up in a sheet! I'd know you anywhere.

EGBERT *(Speaking in a deep, sepulchral tone):* And who do you think I am, my pretty maid?

PIERRETTE: Don't "pretty maid" me! I'm good and angry at you, Bill Templeton. The others have gone on a ghost hunt, and here I am, waiting for you.

EGBERT: A ghost hunt! They don't need to go hunting for a ghost when I'm right here.

PIERRETTE: Stop talking nonsense, and tell me where you've been all this time.

EGBERT *(Spookily):* I've been walking for hours in the realms of the dead.

PIERRETTE: Phooey!

EGBERT: You talk as if you don't believe I'm a real ghost.

PIERRETTE *(Scornfully):* What do you take me for? That isn't a very good disguise. Anybody would know you.

EGBERT: Don't you feel a chill as I approach you? Can't you feel the damp of the grave when I touch you? *(Reaches out to touch her arm)*

PIERRETTE *(Pulling back):* Don't you touch me! You're just trying to avoid the main question, which is why you're so late.

EGBERT: I am not so late. I have till the stroke of midnight to turn you blue with fright.

PIERRETTE: And I'll turn you black and blue if you don't give me some logical explanation of your behavior.

EGBERT: A spirit never explains.

PIERRETTE: O.K., I'm through. If you can't talk like a human being, get out of here.

EGBERT: How can I talk like a human being when I'm a ghost?

PIERRETTE: Take off that ghost mask. False face would describe you better!

EGBERT: I wear no face but my own. *(Sighing)* Why can't I frighten you?

PIERRETTE: You could never frighten me. You're a bigger fraidy cat than I ever was.

EGBERT *(Hanging his head):* Alas, you speak the truth—and this was my last chance.

PIERRETTE *(Irritated):* I think you must have a fever. Let me feel your head.

EGBERT: You'll find my forehead is cold and damp as the tomb.

PIERRETTE: Mildew on the brain, that's what you have.

EGBERT: That settles it. I will not stay here to be insulted. I'll vanish in a blue flame.

PIERRETTE: You'll do nothing of the sort. You'll stay right here, and do the number we promised the kids. We signed up for this floor show act a week ago and that means we're going through with it.

EGBERT: You talk like a mad woman.

PIERRETTE: I *am* a mad woman, mad at you, and as soon as our act is over, I'm going home. *(Talking and laughing are heard from offstage.)* Here they come. Let's get set over at the piano. *(GIRLS re-enter with much laughter. GYPSY is still in the lead. EGBERT and PIERRETTE move over to the piano, taking folding chair.)*

GYPSY: And now, we're going to turn our party over to the Master of Ceremonies, and let him introduce our floor show. Let's give our M. C. a great big hand! *(M.C., wearing tail coat, high silk hat, and pair of gym shorts, moves forward.)*

M.C.: O.K., everyone, find a place on the floor, and get set for the big event of the evening. *(GYPSY and GIRLS sit on floor. Calls off to STAGE HANDS)* Now, if one of you will bring the microphone forward, we'll have the thrill of a lifetime. *(STAGE HANDS enter, bring microphone to enter. Spot up on microphone.)* The management wishes to present the most sensational of all entertainers, that super-colossal heartbreaker, that inimitable moaner and groaner and crooner of tunes and croons, Bill Templeton, "The Voice" of Sheridan High! *(There is loud appluase. M.C. shoves EGBERT into spotlight at microphone. PIERRETTE, at piano, strikes a few opening chords. EGBERT begins an exaggerated crooning number. As he sings, MOTHER and FATHER enter and stand at one side. GIRLS swoon with delight.)*

GIRLS *(Ad lib):* Ooooh! He's divine! I feel faint! *(Etc.)*

M.C.: Atta boy, Bill! You're knocking them out cold!

MOTHER: Look, Henry! Some of the girls are fainting!

FATHER *(Pleased):* He's a natural. *(Proudly)* A chip off the old block.

MOTHER: I told you all he needed was a little confidence.

FATHER *(Happily):* That caterwauling is enough to send the whole crowd into hysterics.

MOTHER: He's better than any wailing banshee I ever heard. *(As* EGBERT *finishes,* M.C. *leads in applause.)*

M.C.: How about a great big hand for "The Voice" of Sheridan High . . . good old Bill Templeton! (BILL TEMPLETON *enters.)*

BILL: Who's taking my name and fame in vain? Who's the guy in the sheet? *(Strides up to* EGBERT*)* What's the idea of stealing my act? Speak up! *(Grabs him by the sheet)* Who are you?

EGBERT *(Giving a wild laugh):* Ha! Ha! Ha! I am the Ghost of Egbert Edwin Edison Engleheart, the third! Ha! Ha! Ha! *(Lights go off, and there are loud screams of terror from* GIRLS. *Then there is a silence, and lights go back on. Only* FATHER, MOTHER, *and* EGBERT *are onstage.)* Mother! Father! What are you doing here?

FATHER: Congratulations, my boy! You really were in top ghost form! Those kids won't stop running and screaming for hours.

MOTHER: It was magnificent, son, simply magnificent! I never knew you had such a blood-curdling voice.

FATHER: At last we can hold our heads up with the best of the spirits. And you can haunt the finest families in two continents. (SILAS P. STATIC *enters. He is wearing street clothes.)*

STATIC: Just a moment, sir. Pardon me for interrupting you, but I have a proposition to make to this young man. My card, sir. *(Hands card to* EGBERT, *who reads it aloud)*

EGBERT *(Reading):* Silas P. Static, Program Director for the Allied Broadcasting Company.

STATIC: I'm scouting for new talent, and I believe this young man has a great future. I'm lucky I happened to be walking by tonight—I know a budding star when I hear one.

FATHER: Now, wait just a minute. That boy was born to haunt people, and haunt people he shall.

MOTHER: Quiet, Henry. Listen to what Mr. Static has to say.

STATIC: Think for a moment, sir, what opportunities he'll have on the air. His voice will carry into millions of homes.

MOTHER: Think of it, Henry, millions of people shivering in the dark, hearing Egbert's name. *(To* EGBERT*)* What do you say, Egbert?

EGBERT *(Eagerly):* I think it's a great idea. After all, there's not much future in ghosting, at least not in the old style. I'd just as soon be a ghost star as anything else.

STATIC *(Shaking* EGBERT's *hand):* Then, that settles it. Come down to my office in the morning and sign the contract . . . two thousand dollars a week and a double bonus every Halloween.

MOTHER *(Happily):* You see, Henry, that's Egbert's reward for being a softhearted ghost. *(Curtain)*

THE END

The Runaway Unicorn

Characters

UNICORN KEEPER
ROBIN HOOD
WILL SCARLET
LITTLE JOHN
ALICE IN WONDERLAND
PINOCCHIO
PETER RABBIT
JACK *(of beanstalk fame)*
SNOW WHITE
THE SEVEN DWARFS
MOTHER GOOSE
HANSEL
GRETEL
THE WIZARD OF OZ
LINDA BORDEN
LEWIS BORDEN
UNICORN

SETTING: *Storybook Lane in Bookland. Onstage are large cardboard posters representing nine books:* ROBIN HOOD, ALICE IN WONDERLAND, PINOCCHIO, PETER RABBIT, MOTHER GOOSE, HANSEL AND GRETEL,

SNOW WHITE, JACK AND THE BEANSTALK, *and* THE
WIZARD OF OZ. *Storybook characters are concealed
behind their posters. Will Scarlett and Little John
stand behind the* ROBIN HOOD *poster. Backdrop shows
Mother Hubbard's house.*

AT RISE: UNICORN KEEPER *runs in from right.*

UNICORN KEEPER: Help! Help! The Unicorn has run
away! Help! Help! We must find him at once! *(Book
characters step out from behind their posters.)*

ROBIN HOOD: Are you sure he's gone?

UNICORN KEEPER: I've looked all over Bookland for him.
He's not anywhere on Storybook Lane.

ALICE: Did you look in Poetry Park? He sometimes goes
there in the afternoon.

UNICORN KEEPER: He's not there now!

GRETEL: Maybe he's lost in the haunted wood!

SNOW WHITE: Maybe he tried to climb the magic moun-
tain.

PINOCCHIO: Maybe he started to swim to Treasure Is-
land.

MOTHER GOOSE *(To* UNICORN KEEPER*):* You were never
strict enough with him. The Old Woman in the Shoe
would know what to do with him.

HANSEL: Yes, she'd give him some broth without any
bread, then give him a spanking and send him to bed!

UNICORN KEEPER: But she'd have to find him first, and I
don't even know where else to look.

PETER RABBIT: Why do you think he ran away? Was he
in any trouble?

UNICORN KEEPER: Not that I know of, but yesterday he
wouldn't eat his dinner.

ALICE: He's been very sad lately.

MOTHER GOOSE: He looked to me as if he might be
catching a cold.

GRETEL: Poor little Unicorn. He's probably frightened and can't find his way home.

MOTHER GOOSE: He had no business running away in the first place.

SNOW WHITE: We must find him before dark.

ROBIN HOOD: We'd better form a searching party.

ALICE: I'll take a look through the looking glass and ask the White Rabbit to search through Wonderland. *(Exits)*

PETER RABBIT: I'll look in Mr. McGregor's garden. He might have fallen asleep under a tree. *(Exits)*

JACK: I'll climb up my beanstalk and scan the countryside. *(Exits)*

PINOCCHIO: I'll round up some of my puppet friends. *(Exits)*

HANSEL: Gretel and I will go through the woods.

GRETEL: Maybe he's hiding in the Gingerbread House. *(Both exit.)*

SNOW WHITE: I'll ask the Seven Dwarfs to join our searching party. *(Exits)*

MOTHER GOOSE: I'd like to help, but I have no one to send. Simple Simon is much too simple. Miss Muffet is afraid of everything, even spiders, and Humpty Dumpty is in no shape to go anywhere.

ROBIN HOOD: Never mind, Mother Goose. You stay here and look after things. I'll take Will Scarlet and Little John, two of my very best men. The minute we find the Unicorn, I'll blow my hunting horn. *(Exits left, as* SNOW WHITE *re-enters right with* THE SEVEN DWARFS. *They cross stage, singing to tune of "Heigh-Ho.")*

DWARFS *(Singing):*

> Search high and low,
> It's off to look we go,

We'll keep on looking all day long,
Heigh-ho, heigh-ho,
Heigh-ho, heigh-ho,
We're looking high and low!
And we will find him, this we know
With a heigh, heigh-ho!

UNICORN KEEPER: Everybody is so kind and helpful! I'm sure they'll find him.

WIZARD OF OZ: Oh, no, they won't!

UNICORN KEEPER *(Upset):* Why not?

WIZARD OF OZ: Because I'm a Wizard, that's why. I know all about catching unicorns.

UNICORN KEEPER: Then why didn't you offer to help?

WIZARD OF OZ: No one asked me. When people ask me no questions, I give them no answers.

UNICORN KEEPER *(Pleading):* Oh, dear, kind Wizard of Oz, I'm asking you now. Do you know where the Unicorn is?

WIZARD OF OZ *(Sharply):* No, of course not, but I do know how to catch him and bring him back.

UNICORN KEEPER: How?

WIZARD OF OZ: In the first place, unicorns are very shy creatures.

UNICORN KEEPER: Yes, yes, I know.

WIZARD OF OZ: In the second place, they are very, very clever.

UNICORN KEEPER: Yes, yes, I know.

WIZARD OF OZ: And in the third place, they can run very, very fast.

UNICORN KEEPER: Yes, yes, I know all that.

WIZARD OF OZ: If you know so much, why don't you catch him yourself?

UNICORN KEEPER: Please excuse me, Mr. Wizard. I don't pretend to know as much as you do about unicorns. . . . Just tell me what to do.

WIZARD OF OZ: You must set a unicorn trap!

UNICORN KEEPER (*Drawing away*): Oh, no! A trap is so cruel! I wouldn't want to hurt him.

WIZARD OF OZ: Who said anything about hurting him? This is a very tender trap, indeed.

UNICORN KEEPER (*Grudgingly*): Very well. How do we begin?

WIZARD OF OZ: We will need a real, live little girl—not a storybook child, but a real one.

UNICORN KEEPER: Where will we find one?

WIZARD OF OZ: In the library, of course. I happen to know there is one right there this very minute.

UNICORN KEEPER: How can we bring her here to Bookland?

WIZARD OF OZ: Shut your eyes, and I'll make some magic that will bring her here at once.

UNICORN KEEPER (*Shutting eyes*): My eyes are shut tight.

WIZARD OF OZ (*Acting out words*):
>   I turn round and round about!
>   I put my hat on inside out!
>   I pull my whiskers, one, two, three!
>   Now open your eyes, and here she'll be!

(LINDA *and* LEWIS *enter.*)

UNICORN KEEPER (*In surprise*): You did it! You did it! But look! There are two children instead of one!

WIZARD OF OZ: I must have turned around too many times. But no matter!

LINDA: Good afternoon. I don't believe we have ever met.

LEWIS: How did we get here?

UNICORN KEEPER: This is Bookland, my friends, and you are on Storybook Lane.

WIZARD OF OZ: I am the Wizard of Oz. I brought you here. This *(Points)* is the Unicorn Keeper. He has a problem, and we want you to help him.

LINDA: My name is Linda Borden.

LEWIS: And I am her brother, Lewis. What do you want us to do?

WIZARD OF OZ: There's nothing *you* can do, Lewis, but we want Linda to help us catch a runaway unicorn.

LEWIS: A runaway unicorn!

LINDA: I don't even know what a unicorn is.

UNICORN KEEPER: This unicorn is the most beautiful beast in Bookland.

WIZARD OF OZ: He has the legs of a deer . . .

UNICORN KEEPER: The tail of a lion . . .

WIZARD OF OZ: And the head and body of a horse.

UNICORN KEEPER *(With gestures):* And he has one, big, long horn growing from the middle of his forehead.

LINDA *(Timidly):* Is he dangerous?

WIZARD OF OZ: Not at all! He's as gentle as a lamb.

LINDA: What must I do?

WIZARD OF OZ: Just sit right here in the chair and wait till he comes.

LEWIS: How do you know he'll come?

WIZARD OF OZ: Because the only way to catch a unicorn is to have a pretty little girl stay all alone, and the unicorn will come and lie down at her feet.

UNICORN KEEPER: Please, Linda, will you do it?

LEWIS: Go ahead, Linda. We'll all be nearby so nothing can hurt you.

LINDA: Very well! I'll do it!

ALL: Good! Good!

WIZARD OF OZ: Now, get Linda something to read while she's waiting. *(To* LINDA*)* Sit down right here, Linda. *(Points to chair.* LINDA *sits.)*

UNICORN KEEPER: I know the very book! *(Calling)* Mother Goose! Mother Goose! Come quickly and bring your book of rhymes.

MOTHER GOOSE *(Entering with book):* Here I am, with the book. Who wants it?

UNICORN KEEPER: This is Linda Borden. She's going to help us get our Unicorn back.

MOTHER GOOSE *(To* LEWIS*):* And who's this boy?

WIZARD OF OZ: This is her brother, Lewis. We all would like to wait in your house until the Unicorn returns.

MOTHER GOOSE: Come right in, and I'll see what Mother Hubbard has in her cupboard for this little boy. *(Handing* LINDA *book)* Here you are, Linda. The story of the Unicorn is on page ten. *(All except* LINDA *follow* MOTHER GOOSE *behind house backdrop.)*

LINDA *(Leafing through book):* I'm not so sure I like this. *(Looking at book)* Oh, here's a picture of a unicorn, and he's just as beautiful as they said he was. His body is white, his head is red and his eyes are blue. And what a lovely horn—black in the middle and red at the tip. In the picture he's fighting with a lion. I'm sure the story is exciting. *(Reading)*

> "The Lion and the Unicorn
> Were fighting for the crown,
> The Lion beat the Unicorn
> All round the town."

(Looking up) That's why the unicorn ran away. *(Reading)*

> "Some gave them white bread,
> And some gave them brown,
> Some gave them plum cake,
> And sent them out of town."

(As LINDA *reads,* UNICORN *enters and lies at her feet.)* And after that, he must have come here to live.

UNICORN: That's right, my beautiful lady. That's just what I did.

LINDA: The Unicorn! He's back! (MOTHER GOOSE, UNICORN KEEPER, WIZARD OF OZ, *and* LEWIS *enter.*)

WIZARD OF OZ: It worked, just as I said.

UNICORN KEEPER: My beautiful Unicorn is back safe and sound!

LEWIS: What a wonderful creature! (ROBIN HOOD *enters with* WILL SCARLET *and* LITTLE JOHN.)

ROBIN HOOD: We searched the greenwood, but he wasn't there.

WILL SCARLET: We looked behind every bush and tree!

LITTLE JOHN (*Suddenly seeing* UNICORN; *pointing excitedly*): Quick, Master Robin, blow your horn! There he is!

ROBIN HOOD: He's back! He's back! The search is over! (*As* ROBIN HOOD *blows his horn,* ALICE, HANSEL, GRETEL, JACK, PETER RABBIT, PINOCCHIO *enter.*)

ALICE: I couldn't find him anywhere in Wonderland or Through the Looking Glass.

HANSEL *and* GRETEL: He wasn't in the Gingerbread House.

JACK: I couldn't even spot him from my beanstalk.

PETER RABBIT: And he wasn't in Mr. McGregor's garden!

PINOCCHIO: And my puppet friends and I had no luck, either. (SNOW WHITE *enters with* SEVEN DWARFS.)

SEVEN DWARFS (*Singing to the tune of* "Heigh-Ho"):
> Not high, not low,
> We simply do not know
> Just where that Unicorn did go,
> Did go, did go.
> Heigh-ho, heigh-ho,
> Now we are feeling low,

He positively can't be found
Not high, not low!

SNOW WHITE *(Suddenly):* Look! Look! He's here!

DWARFS *(In unison):* He's here!

PINOCCHIO: But I want to know where he's been.

JACK: And why did he run away?

UNICORN KEEPER: Tell us, my pretty pet. Where have you been?

UNICORN: I've been to my secret hiding place, and where it is, I'll never, never, never tell.

LEWIS: Everybody should have a secret hiding place.

UNICORN KEEPER: But why did you run away and scare us so?

UNICORN: I'm sorry you were so worried, but I can't tell you why I ran away.

LINDA *(Putting her arm around* UNICORN's *neck):* Please, you nice Unicorn, you can tell me.

UNICORN: All right. But I must whisper in your ear. *(Whispers to* LINDA*)*

MOTHER GOOSE: What did he say?

LINDA *(To* UNICORN*):* Is it all right to tell? *(*UNICORN *nods "yes," and* LINDA *turns to book characters.)* He says he ran away because he found out he isn't real!

UNICORN KEEPER: What does he mean?

WIZARD OF OZ: How did he discover this?

LINDA *(Consulting with* UNICORN*):* How did you find out? *(*UNICORN *whispers.)* He says he looked himself up in the dictionary, and it said a unicorn is just a creature out of a storybook.

BOOK CHARACTERS *(Ad lib):* But so are we. We're all storybook characters. *(Etc.)*

PINOCCHIO *(Sadly):* I'm just a puppet carved from a block of wood.

PETER RABBIT: I was made up by an English woman named Beatrix Potter.

HANSEL *and* GRETEL: We were also made up by the Brothers Grimm.

ROBIN HOOD: Most of my adventures were made up!

MOTHER GOOSE: I'm not real, either, but I never lose any sleep over it.

WIZARD OF OZ: Even I, the great Wizard of Oz, stepped right out of a book, written by Frank Baum.

LEWIS: Even if you did step out of a storybook, you're real to me.

UNICORN *(Puzzled):* What do you mean? I don't understand.

LINDA: You are real to all of the children who read about you in books.

LEWIS: When they read about you, they believe in you and love you, and that makes you real to them.

UNICORN: Is that true?

LINDA: Absolutely.

UNICORN: Oh, how wonderful!

WIZARD OF OZ: You two are very clever children. Very clever indeed!

LEWIS: That's because we spend so much time in the library.

LINDA: And read so many books. When we go home, we're going to tell all of our friends to read about *(Points to each one in turn)* Mother Goose, and Hansel and Gretel, and Snow White, and Jack in the Beanstalk.

LEWIS: And Robin Hood and Peter Rabbit and Pinocchio and the Wizard of Oz! *(Turns)* And you, of course, Unicorn.

UNICORN: You won't forget me? (MOTHER GOOSE *exits*

as LINDA *moves to Unicorn.)*

LINDA *(Hugging* UNICORN*):* We'll never forget you.

UNICORN: I'm so happy! I'll never run away again! *(*MOTHER GOOSE *re-enters, carrying a crown.)*

MOTHER GOOSE: To show you how glad we are to have you home again, Unicorn, I have a present for you. *(Puts crown on* UNICORN's *head)* Now you won't have to fight the lion for the crown. You have one of your very own.

UNICORN: Thank you! Thank you!

MOTHER GOOSE: From now on, there'll be another verse printed in my book. *(Recites)*

> The Lion and the Unicorn
> Were fighting for the crown,
> But our friendly unicorn
> Is ruler of the town.

ALL: Long live King Unicorn! Hurray! Hurray! Hurray! *(Curtain)*

THE END

Thanks to Butter-Fingers

Characters

MRS. UPTON, *a collector of antiques*
DEAN, *her teenage son*
CHARLOTTE, *her ten-year-old daughter*
BETSY, *her ten-year-old niece*
DR. RINEHART, *an antique expert*

TIME: *Thanksgiving Day.*
SETTING: *The Upton dining room. At center is large table covered with a cloth. Chairs are placed around the table. Small side table is nearby; electric coffeepot is set on it. China closet is against upstage wall.*
AT RISE: MRS. UPTON *and* CHARLOTTE *are arranging the centerpiece of fruit and autumn leaves on table.* DEAN, *who wears glasses, is repairing electric coffeepot. Suddenly, there is a loud crash offstage.*
MRS. UPTON: Good grief! What has your cousin Betsy broken now?
CHARLOTTE: If she stays much longer, we won't have a dish left.
MRS. UPTON: Charlotte, remember, she's our guest. *(Shakes her head)* But I must admit I never saw such a butter-fingers!

DEAN: Why are you two always picking on Betsy, Mom? She's a good kid.

MRS. UPTON: We're not picking on her, Dean. And she is a lovely girl. But you'll have to admit she does break things.

DEAN: But, Mom, you know she just wants to help. With Aunt Frances and Uncle Bill in Europe, I guess she feels pretty homesick, especially at Thanksgiving. (BETSY *enters, carrying stack of plates.*)

BETSY (*Cheerfully*): Did you hear that crash, Aunt Martha? I just dropped the bag of potatoes and knocked the frying pan off the stove. Nothing broke.

MRS. UPTON: So that's what it was! Now, Betsy, put down those plates before you drop them.

CHARLOTTE: You shouldn't carry so many at one time. After all, they're Mommy's best china.

BETSY: Well, I didn't drop a single one. (*Trips slightly but manages to place plates safely on the table*) What can I do now, Aunt Martha?

MRS. UPTON: Why don't you start peeling the potatoes, while Charlotte and I finish the table?

BETSY: But, Aunt Martha, I hate to peel potatoes, and these dishes are so beautiful. Please let me help set the table. I promise to be careful.

DEAN: Give her a break, Mom.

MRS. UPTON: All right. I guess you can put out the silver. It's in the kitchen. Charlotte, you can bring the tray of glassware. Be careful, now.

CHARLOTTE: O.K., Mom. (CHARLOTTE *and* BETSY *exit.*)

MRS. UPTON: I guess everything will work out. Betsy goes back to school Monday. I only hope she and Charlotte can manage to stay friends that long.

They've fought like cats and dogs ever since they were little.

DEAN: I guess they're just jealous of each other, Mom.

MRS. UPTON: Jealous? What on earth would they have to be jealous of?

DEAN: Don't ask me. But you know how girls are. *(CHARLOTTE and BETSY enter, each with a tray.)*

BETSY: Here we are, Aunt Martha, and I didn't drop a single spoon.

MRS. UPTON *(To CHARLOTTE)*: Careful with the tray, dear. I wouldn't want anything to happen to those glasses. *(Both girls set down trays.)*

BETSY: You have such beautiful dishes, Aunt Martha.

MRS. UPTON: I'm glad you like them, Betsy. These are antiques, and they can't be replaced.

DEAN: Then why are we using them, Mom? These antiques of yours always make me nervous.

MRS. UPTON: We're using them because it's a holiday, and Dr. Rinehart is coming for dinner. Now I really must check the turkey. *(Exits)*

BETSY: Who is Dr. Rinehart?

DEAN *(Sarcastically)*: Oh, he's some sort of antique expert that knows all about cracked sugar bowls and teapots.

CHARLOTTE: Don't be silly, Dean. Dr. Rinehart writes articles for magazines and takes photos of beautiful table settings. Mom is just dying to have him take some pictures of our dishes. And besides, she thinks he might want to feature the bride sugar bowl in his exhibit.

BETSY *(With great interest)*: The bride sugar bowl! What in the world is that?

DEAN: Just an old sugar bowl that looks like a cross

between a wash bowl and a coffeepot.

CHARLOTTE: Don't believe a thing he says, Betsy. The bride sugar bowl is over two hundred years old. It was brought over from England by the first Upton family who came to America.

BETSY: But why is it called the bride sugar bowl?

CHARLOTTE: Because it's always been handed down to the first bride in the family.

BETSY: Isn't that romantic! Where is it? I'd love to see it.

CHARLOTTE: It's in the china closet . . . way in the back. *(As* BETSY *runs toward closet)* You'll see it later. Nobody's allowed to touch it but Mom.

DEAN: You might as well tell her the rest of the story— all about the Southern bride who disappeared during the Civil War.

CHARLOTTE: That was our great grandmother's sister, Delia. When their farm was burned, she escaped with the sugar bowl.

BETSY: You mean the sugar bowl was the only thing she saved out of the whole house?

DEAN: That's all. Everything else was destroyed. Now the old sugar bowl's safe and sound in our china closet. It's a real museum piece.

BETSY *(Scornfully)*: It all sounds sort of corny to me.

CHARLOTTE: Corny? What do you mean by corny?

BETSY: Well, don't you think it was sort of dumb of your ancestor to save a silly thing like a sugar bowl?

DEAN: Remember, Betsy, she's *your* ancestor, too, you know.

BETSY: She is?

DEAN: Of course. We're both Uptons, aren't we? Grandpa Upton had two sons, your dad and ours.

BETSY *(With new interest)*: You mean I'm part owner of the sugar bowl?

CHARLOTTE *(Heatedly):* Of course not! It belongs to Mom.

DEAN: Actually, Charlotte, it belongs to Dad. Grandma got the sugar bowl when she was a bride. Since she had no daughters, she gave it to the first son who brought home a bride, and that was Dad.

CHARLOTTE: And Dad will give it to me when I am a bride.

BETSY: How do you know? If the first bride in the family gets the sugar bowl, how do you know it won't be me?

DEAN *(Laughing):* There's a point you never figured on, did you, Charlotte?

CHARLOTTE *(Upset):* But you couldn't get the sugar bowl. It belongs to me! Mom always said it would be mine when I get married, Betsy. How dare you say it will be yours?

DEAN: Oh, good grief! You're still kids, and you're fighting about who will be the first bride.

CHARLOTTE: But she won't! She won't be the first bride!

DEAN *(Laughing):* O.K., you two can fight it out. I'm going downstairs for an extension cord. *(Exits)*

BETSY: Just what makes you so sure I couldn't be a bride as quick as you, Charlotte Upton? I'm quicker at everything else. I can jump rope faster than you, and I can swim faster and run faster, and . . .

CHARLOTTE: Is that so? Well, getting married has nothing to do with jumping or swimming. You drop everything you touch. You're just a butter-fingers.

BETSY: Who said I was a butter-fingers?

CHARLOTTE: My own mother said so.

BETSY: I don't believe you. Aunt Martha likes to have me here. She told Mother she did.

CHARLOTTE: Well, she doesn't like to have you break all our dishes.

BETSY *(Upset):* I never broke a single dish—just a lamp and two flower vases. And I don't believe Aunt Martha ever said that.

CHARLOTTE: She did, too. So there.

BETSY *(Doubling up her fist and starting toward* CHARLOTTE*):* Charlotte Upton, if you're making this up . . .

CHARLOTTE: Don't you dare touch me, don't you dare! *(Takes glass from tray, as if planning to throw it. It slips out of her hand and breaks.)*

BETSY *(Triumphantly):* There! See what you did? You broke that glass!

CHARLOTTE: It slipped! It was an accident! Oh, no! It's one of Mother's real crystal goblets. *(*MRS. UPTON *enters.)*

MRS. UPTON: How are you two getting along? Is the table ready? *(Sees the broken glass on floor)* Oh, Betsy, how on earth did you manage to break this? I distinctly told you to put out the silver and keep your hands off the glass and china.

BETSY: But Aunt Martha, I . . .

MRS. UPTON *(Angrily):* You're a regular little butter-fingers! Charlotte, go get the dustpan and broom and help me sweep this up. *(*CHARLOTTE *exits.)* Betsy, you might as well go to your room and stay there till it's time for dinner. And while you're there, change your dress and comb your hair. We're having a guest for dinner, remember?

BETSY: Yes, Aunt Martha.

MRS. UPTON: And try not to touch anything breakable in the bedroom. *(Calling)* Charlotte, hurry up with that broom and dustpan. I'll see what's keeping her. *(Exits)*

BETSY *(Bursting into tears):* I didn't break that old

glass! I'm not a butter-fingers. I'll show them! They'll be sorry they ever called me butter-fingers! *(Rushes out left, sobbing.* MRS. UPTON *and* CHARLOTTE *re-enter, right, carrying dustpan and broom.* MRS. UPTON *begins to sweep glass into dustpan* CHARLOTTE *holds.)*

MRS. UPTON: Now my set is broken.

CHARLOTTE *(Slowly):* Mom, I don't think you should blame Betsy for breaking the glass. It was . . . well . . . it was an accident.

MRS. UPTON: Of course, dear. They're all accidents. I'm sure she doesn't go around breaking things on purpose. But that doesn't make me feel any better about my glass.

CHARLOTTE *(Glumly):* No, I suppose not.

MRS. UPTON: There! I guess we got it all. Now please dump it in the rubbish, and then come back and finish setting the table. I have to go pick up Dr. Rinehart. Please, dear, try to keep Betsy from having any more accidents till I get back.

CHARLOTTE *(Meekly):* I'll try, Mom. *(*MRS. UPTON *and* CHARLOTTE *exit in opposite directions. After a brief pause,* DEAN *enters, carrying long narrow piece of plywood and an extension cord.)*

DEAN: Well, girls, have you decided who's going to be the first Upton bride? *(Sees the room is empty, shrugs)* I wonder where everyone is? Oh, well. Maybe this board will fix this wobbly antique table. *(Puts board on chair and crawls under table with extension cord. He is almost completely out of sight.)* Now why are electric outlets always in such impossible places? *(*BETSY *enters, with large jar of cold cream. She doesn't see* DEAN.*)*

BETSY: *Butter-fingers*, am I? Well, I'll show them who's a *butter-fingers*. (*Crosses to table, starts putting plates and glasses around at place settings. Surveys her work*) Um-m! Very nice, if I do say so myself! Miss Butter-Fingers didn't drop a single glass or plate! (DEAN *crawls partly out from under table and watches her.* BETSY *opens jar and begins greasing the bottom of each plate and glass.*) I think this cocoa butter will do the trick. (*Giggles*) I can hardly wait till they start passing their plates up to Uncle Harry. (DEAN *emerges from under table.*)

DEAN: So you can't wait, can you? Well, here's something I just can't wait to do to you. (*Picks up piece of plywood and brandishes it*)

BETSY: Please, Dean. Give me a chance to explain.

DEAN: You'd better talk fast. What's the idea of greasing all those dishes?

BETSY: To make the rest of you know how it feels to be called a butter-fingers.

DEAN: And break all of Mom's good dishes, just like you broke the other stuff?

BETSY: But I didn't break it all, Dean. Not the glass.

DEAN: What glass?

BETSY: The glass that Charlotte broke and blamed on me.

DEAN: Charlotte did that?

BETSY: Well, she didn't exactly say I broke it, but she didn't say *she* did, so naturally Aunt Martha thought it was butter-fingers again.

DEAN: I see. And just where is my sweet sister right now?

BETSY: I don't know. (*Upset*) I didn't mean to tell on her. Charlotte hates me, and Aunt Martha says I'm a butter-fingers, and now you hate me, too.

DEAN: No, I don't, Betsy. And you know what? I think I know why you're a butter-fingers.

BETSY: Why? Just because I'm careless?

DEAN *(Laughing):* Not at all. I think you need a pair of glasses—just like mine. Betsy, when I was in the fifth grade the guys made fun of me because I could never hit the ball. But the trouble was my eyes. I think that's your problem, too. The trouble is not with your fingers, but your eyes.

BETSY: Oh, Dean, do you really think so?

DEAN: Yes. As soon as your Mother and Dad come back from Europe, ask them to take you to the eye doctor.

BETSY: I will! And I'm really sorry about the plates. I'll wipe them off right away, and nobody will ever know. *(CHARLOTTE enters. When she sees DEAN and BETSY, she stops short.)*

CHARLOTTE *(To BETSY):* I thought you were supposed to be in your room.

DEAN *(Firmly):* She's right where she's supposed to be. Charlotte, sit down in this chair for a moment.

CHARLOTTE: Why should I?

DEAN: Because I want to talk to you about a certain sister of mine who would let her cousin take the blame for a glass she broke.

CHARLOTTE *(Turning to BETSY):* Why, you little tattletale!

DEAN *(Seizing CHARLOTTE by the arm and pushing her into a chair):* Quiet. We've had enough name-calling in this house. Ever since you two were tiny you've fought every time you've been together. You fought over toys, games, and today you even fought over a sugar bowl. This is the end. Thanksgiving is for families, and families should like each other, be grateful for each other.

CHARLOTTE *(Angrily):* I'm not grateful for her! She's spoiled my whole Thanksgiving and made me break one of Mother's glasses.

BETSY *(Shouting):* I'm not grateful for you, either. You called me a butter-fingers, and—and—

DEAN *(Firmly):* I'm giving you two exactly five minutes to come up with five good reasons why you're thankful for each other. So start thinking.

CHARLOTTE: I couldn't think of five reasons in five months.

BETSY: It would take me five years.

DEAN: That's too bad. *(Looking at his watch)* You have four and a half minutes left.

BETSY: I think he means it, Charlotte. We'd better get started.

CHARLOTTE *(In a wail):* But I can't think of any reason to be thankful for you.

BETSY: I'm going to try. *(Shuts her eyes for a moment, then opens them)* How much time do we have left?

DEAN: Not much.

BETSY: O.K. I'm ready. I'm thankful I have a cousin with such beautiful blue eyes and blond hair.

CHARLOTTE: That's no fair. You told me yesterday you hated my blond hair.

BETSY *(Shyly):* I know. But I never really hated it. I guess I said I did because I'd rather have blond hair than these dark pigtails.

CHARLOTTE *(Smiling):* Do you really mean that?

BETSY: Yes, I do.

CHARLOTTE: I'm thankful I have a cousin who is so good at games and always comes in first at all the races.

BETSY: I thought you hated games. You always said they weren't ladylike.

CHARLOTTE: I said that because I couldn't do them. I'm

the slowest runner in the whole school.

BETSY *(Smiling):* This isn't hard at all. I'm thankful I have a cousin who is always so neat and clever around the house. I'm never allowed to do anything at home except make beds and peel potatoes.

CHARLOTTE: I'm thankful I have a cousin who isn't afraid to climb trees and doesn't mind getting dirty or tearing her dresses. I think she must lead an exciting life.

BETSY *(Sighing):* Not very exciting. Just messy. I'm thankful I have a cousin to stay with on Thanksgiving, when my parents are away from home.

CHARLOTTE *(Happily):* This is beginning to be fun. I'm thankful I have a cousin who visits me, because we can do things together. It's almost like having a sister.

BETSY: How are we doing, Dean?

DEAN: Fine. You have two more to go.

BETSY: O.K. I'm thankful I have a cousin who is going to be the first bride of the Upton family . . . and get the family sugar bowl.

DEAN: Hey, this is going a bit too far.

BETSY: No, it isn't. For number five, I'm thankful I have a cousin who made us realize we should start appreciating each other.

CHARLOTTE: And I'm thankful I have a cousin who is such a good sport about everything, including her butter-fingers.

DEAN *(In a warning tone):* Charlotte!

BETSY *(Laughing):* I don't care, Dean. That doesn't make me mad any longer, now that Charlotte and I are friends.

DEAN: All right. Now, you two get busy and wipe the cocoa butter off those plates. I'm going to finish fixing this table. *(Crawls under table with piece of wood)*

CHARLOTTE: Cocoa butter? I don't understand.

BETSY: I was trying to make butter-fingers of all of you by greasing the plates with cocoa butter. Come on and help me wipe it off before Aunt Martha and Dr. Rinehart get here.

CHARLOTTE: I'll get a cloth. *(Exits)*

BETSY *(To DEAN):* I'll never forget this Thanksgiving, Dean. *(CHARLOTTE enters with two dish towels. Girls wipe the plates and glasses quickly.)* Doesn't the table look pretty?

CHARLOTTE: Beautiful. I hope Dr. Rinehart thinks so.

DEAN *(Coming out from under the table):* There, that does it for the table. It's perfectly level. *(MRS. UPTON enters, followed by DR. RINEHART, who carries a flash camera.)*

MRS. UPTON *(Removing coat and taking DR. RINEHART's coat):* Here we are, Dr. Rinehart. This is my son Dean. *(They acknowledge introductions.)* Dean, will you take our coats upstairs, please? *(DEAN exits with coats.)* And this is my niece, Betsy, whose parents are in England.

BETSY: Good afternoon, Dr. Rinehart.

DR. RINEHART: Hello, Betsy.

MRS. UPTON: And, of course, you already know my daughter, Charlotte.

DR. RINEHART: Happy Thanksgiving, Charlotte. Did you help set this gorgeous table?

CHARLOTTE: Betsy helped me, Dr. Rinehart. *(MRS. UPTON looks at CHARLOTTE in surprise.)*

DR. RINEHART: And do you like antique dishes, Betsy?

BETSY: I think they're beautiful, sir, but I don't know very much about them. I never even heard of the bride sugar bowl until today. *(DEAN re-enters.)*

DR. RINEHART: Ah, yes, the bride sugar bowl. That is the piece I've been hoping to borrow and photograph for our Early American Exhibit, Mrs. Upton. I'm so anxious to see it.

MRS. UPTON: It's right here in the china closet. *(To* DEAN*)* Will you get it down, please, dear?

DEAN: Not me! Suppose I drop it?

MRS. UPTON: You won't, and you're tall enough to reach it. *(*DEAN *gets sugar bowl from closet and hands it to* DR. RINEHART, *who inspects it carefully.)*

DR. RINEHART: Beautiful! Beautiful! Exquisite! As perfect a piece as I have ever seen, Mrs. Upton. You realize, of course, that this piece is worth quite a sum?

MRS. UPTON: Oh, yes, but we'd never dream of letting it go out of the family. You see, the tradition is that it always goes to the first Upton bride. Since we have only two girls in the family, it will go to either Charlotte or Betsy.

DR. RINEHART: I must say they're a bit young to be thinking of that right now. *(Smiling)* But since you are the heiresses apparent, how would you like to be photographed holding the precious bowl?

CHARLOTTE: But I'm never allowed to touch it.

BETSY: I'd be frightened to death to as much as breathe on it.

MRS. UPTON: Nonsense, girls. If Dr. Rinehart wants to take a picture, it will be all right.

CHARLOTTE: But it *would* be dreadful to break it now, after all it's been through.

DR. RINEHART *(Posing girls):* Now, girls, stand right here in front of the table, holding the bowl like this. *(Gives bowl to* CHARLOTTE*)*

BETSY *(Picking up the lid by the knob):* Maybe I could be looking inside like this . . . *(Drops lid. Everyone screams.)*

MRS. UPTON *(Clutching a chair, her eyes closed):* I can't

bear to look. Is it still in one piece?

DR. RINEHART *(Scrambling around on the floor):* I regret to say, Mrs. Upton, the knob and lid are now two pieces.

MRS. UPTON: Ruined! That beautiful piece is absolutely ruined! *(Angrily)* Betsy! Betsy! How could you?

CHARLOTTE *(Setting bowl on table and putting her arms around BETSY):* It wasn't Betsy's fault, Mother. She barely lifted the lid, and the knob came off.

DEAN: Let me see those pieces. *(Picks up knob and lid)*

BETSY: Oh, Dean, I *am* a butter-fingers. It wasn't my eyes this time. It just fell out of my hand.

DEAN: I know it did, Betsy. And do you know why? Because this lid had been broken long before you ever touched it. Look at the knob. You can see little pieces of gritty cement around the edges.

DR. RINEHART: Nonsense! I would have detected it. That was a perfect piece.

DEAN: Sorry to disagree, Dr. Rinehart, but that sugar bowl lid had been mended ages ago. The cement or glue or whatever was used had dried out, and when Betsy picked it up, the knob and lid came apart. *(Leaning over suddenly and picking ring up from the floor)* And if you don't believe me, here's the proof.

ALL *(Crowding round):* What? What is it?

CHARLOTTE: It's a diamond ring!

MRS. UPTON: Where did it come from?

DR. RINEHART *(Examining the ring):* It's a fabulous antique setting. Whose is it?

MRS. UPTON: I have no idea.

DEAN: I have. It must have belonged to the bride who saved the sugar bowl from the great fire. She wasn't saving the sugar bowl. She was saving her ring.

DR. RINEHART: Young man, you really have something

there. She doubtless concealed her most valuable and cherished possession by sealing it between the knob and the lid of the sugar bowl.

BETSY: And no one ever knew it was there.

CHARLOTTE: And we wouldn't know it yet if it hadn't been for Betsy.

DR. RINEHART: If this ring is worth what I think it is, you owe her a vote of thanks.

MRS. UPTON: Betsy, dear, you gave us a bad scare, but we're certainly grateful for it.

DR. RINEHART: What a story this will make in my magazine.

DEAN: What a story this has already made! Let's get on with the picture-taking, Dr. Rinehart. I'm beginning to get hungry.

MRS. UPTON: Yes, it is getting late. It's almost time to start on that turkey.

DR. RINEHART: All right. Which of the girls wants to display the ring?

CHARLOTTE: Let Betsy wear it. After all, she's responsible for the discovery.

MRS. UPTON: That's a good idea, Charlotte. *(Puts ring on* BETSY's *finger)* Here, dear, here's your first chance to wear the family heirloom. Maybe some day you'll wear it for keeps.

BETSY: Oh, thank you, Aunt Martha. I never knew I'd live to see the day I'd be thankful for being a butter-fingers.

CHARLOTTE: And thanks to butter-fingers, and to Dean, Betsy and I have discovered that the best part of Thanksgiving is being thankful for each other. *(Curtain)*

THE END

Pilgrim Parting

Characters

MASTER CHILTON, *a Pilgrim father*
MISTRESS CHILTON, *a Pilgrim mother*
MILES CHILTON, *their son*
COMFORT CHILTON, *their daughter*
SAILOR HUMPHREY, *of the* Mayflower *crew*
MASTER JONES, *Captain of the* Mayflower
SQUANTO, *an Indian friend*
JOHN CARVER, *Governor of Plymouth*
WILLIAM BRADFORD, *author of the Mayflower Compact*
ELDER BREWSTER, *a leader of Plymouth*
JOHN ALDEN
PRISCILLA MULLENS
MISTRESS HOPKINS
MISTRESS BRADFORD
MEN ⎫
WOMEN ⎬ *extras*
CHILDREN ⎭

TIME: *Early morning of April 5, 1621.*
SETTING: *Beach in Plymouth, Massachusetts. There may be some boxes and trunks to one side and some driftwood, if desired. Backdrop shows sea and sky.*

AT RISE: MISTRESS MARY *and* MASTER JOHN CHILTON *enter.* MASTER CHILTON *carries a small sea chest.* MISTRESS MARY *carries two cloaks over her arm and a covered basket.*

MASTER CHILTON: This chest is not too heavy. Have you packed all the children's things?

MISTRESS CHILTON: Everything but these cloaks. Comfort and Miles will need them when they are out at sea.

MASTER CHILTON: And the provisions?

MISTRESS CHILTON: This basket is filled to the brim. *(She puts basket down.)*

MASTER CHILTON: We'll turn the basket over to Master Jones. He'll give them food as they need it.

MISTRESS CHILTON *(Pointing off):* Just look how lightly the *Mayflower* rides the waves.

MASTER CHILTON: Aye. The London merchants will be vexed when they discover she comes home without a cargo. *(Looks off)* The men have loaded her with stones for ballast, but even so, she sits high in the water.

MISTRESS CHILTON: I sometimes wish we were going back with Miles and Comfort. 'Tis hard to part with them; they are so young.

MASTER CHILTON: Aye, Mary, but we have set our hopes in this new land. Cousin Allen and his wife will give them a good home. Miles will have his schooling, and Comfort will be taught what a housewife should know.

MISTRESS CHILTON: At least they will be safe from sickness. Think of it, John, fifteen of the twenty-one boys in the Colony have died in the last year.

MASTER CHILTON *(Shaking his head):* It has been a dreadful winter. But all that is behind us now. Spring and summer are ahead.

MISTRESS CHILTON: And after that, another winter.

(Sighing) At least Comfort and Miles won't have to endure another one. But I am afraid they are upset at leaving. Comfort weeps at night, and Miles looks like a thundercloud. They would prefer to stay.

MASTER CHILTON: It is not for them to decide. *(Abruptly)* Come, Mary, we had better go back to the house and waken them. There is still much to be done before the *Mayflower* sails.

MISTRESS CHILTON: It will seem strange not to see the familiar outline of the *Mayflower.* She is our last link with home.

MASTER CHILTON: Come, before we are overtaken with homesickness. *(Looks off)* Look, here comes Sailor Humphrey. He can take the chest down the shallop. *(SAILOR HUMPHREY enters.)* Good day to you, sir. 'Tis a fine day you have for sailing.

HUMPHREY: Aye, sir. That it is. *(Points)* Are these parcels for the *Mayflower?*

MISTRESS CHILTON: Aye. The basket is filled with provisions, so please take care to keep it upright.

HUMPHREY: Aye, ma'am. Are the children ready for the voyage?

MISTRESS CHILTON: Aye, but they're unhappy to leave this place.

HUMPHREY: Humph! They do not know how lucky they are to be getting back to civilization. Their elders would do well to climb aboard with them.

MASTER CHILTON: You may be right in some ways. But this land has a strange hold on you, once you've weathered a winter here.

HUMPHREY: Too strange for me to understand, sir. I can only understand that I'm heading back to good, old England.

MISTRESS CHILTON: I trust you'll keep an eye on our children.

HUMPHREY: Aye, ma'am. Master Jones and I will see that they come to no harm.

MASTER CHILTON: Thank you, sir, and good morning. Come, Mary. (MISTRESS *and* MASTER CHILON *exit.* HUMPHREY *picks up chest, basket, and cloaks.*)

HUMPHREY *(To himself):* My pockets be bulging already with messages and parcels for folks back in England. *(Sniffs at basket)* Um-m! Mistress Chilton must have tucked some tasty goodies in this basket. *(Starts off.* MILES *and* COMFORT *enter.)*

MILES: Wait! Please wait, Sailor Humphrey.

HUMPHREY: Bless my buttons, if it isn't our two little passengers! Good morning to you, my mates. *(Sets down basket and chest)*

COMFORT: Good morning to you, sir. May we please have our cloaks?

MILES: And the basket?

HUMPHREY: Nay, nay, children. These parcels weigh like a feather on my shoulder.

MILES: But it isn't that, sir. . . .

COMFORT: It's our cloaks. We . . . we want to wear them.

HUMPHREY: Surely you'll not be needing your cloaks on a fine morning like this.

MILES: And the basket, sir. We . . . well, you see, we haven't had breakfast.

HUMPHREY *(Laughing):* That I understand. But I just saw your parents heading off towards home. Perhaps you'd better run back to the house and fill your stomachs with a home-cooked meal.

MILES: But . . . we don't want any breakfast. You see,

we just—well, please, we must have that basket.

COMFORT: And the cloaks, too. It will be cold in the forest. *(Stops abruptly)*

HUMPHREY: The forest? What is this about the forest?

MILES *(Angrily):* I told you to hold your tongue, Comfort. Now you've given our plan away.

HUMPHREY: What plan are you thinking of, Miles? Whatever it is, I have a notion your father and mother know naught of it.

MILES: Oh, please, Sailor Humphrey. Please, help us! All we ask is that you give us our cloaks and the basket of food.

COMFORT: So that we do not die of cold and starvation.

HUMPHREY *(Sitting on chest):* Now what do you intend to do? You will be safely on your way to England in less than an hour.

MILES *(Firmly):* But that's just it—we're not going.

HUMPHREY: Not going?

MILES: No. We're running away.

COMFORT: And hiding in the woods until the ship is safely out of sight.

HUMPHREY *(Whistling in surprise):* So that's what you're up to, is it? And what do you think your father will do when he finds you?

MILES: I don't want to think about that just now, sir. But nothing he could do would make the *Mayflower* come back. No matter how we are punished, we'll be able to stay here in Plymouth.

HUMPHREY *(Shaking his head):* Your head must be addled, to risk the dangers of the forest and your father's anger to stay in this miserable spot.

COMFORT *(Defiantly):* It's not a miserable spot, sir, and we wish to grow up here. One of these days you will see a fair town on this spot with streets and towers and steeples, like those you see in London.

HUMPHREY: I'm not waiting for that, miss. Once I set foot on England's soil again, I'll make no more voyages to the New World.

MILES: Please, sir, we do not have time for talk. In a few minutes, everyone will be coming down to the shore to see the *Mayflower* sail.

HUMPHREY: And in a few moments I plan to have you two on board where you belong. *(Stands)*

COMFORT: There's no persuading him, Miles. We'll have to go without our cloaks and without the food.

MILES: Surely you can understand, sir. You told me yourself how you ran away from home and went to sea when you were only a lad. Surely what we are doing is not as bad as that.

COMFORT: We are only running away so we can stay at home.

MILES: And we will be with our parents. No matter how angry Father may be, he will forgive us!

COMFORT: And Mother will be happy. She was crying last night at the thought of our leaving.

HUMPHREY: You are a fine pair with words, I must admit. *(Scratches his head)* True, I did run away to sea when I was less than your age. But . . .

COMFORT: Please, Sailor Humphrey, please help us. *(HUMPHREY hands them cloaks and basket.)*

HUMPHREY: Very well! I'll help ye—though I may walk the plank for it. *(Picks up chest)* This chest I'll put in the shallop according to orders. Now make yourselves scarce before we're all in trouble.

COMFORT: Oh, thank you! thank you!

MILES: We'll have to run for it, Comfort. Any moment now, they'll discover we've gone.

HUMPHREY *(In warning tone):* If you lose your scalps

before sunset, it's no fault of mine.

COMFORT: The Indians have signed a pledge. Massasoit will not let his people harm us, and we will not harm his people.

HUMPHREY *(Scornfully):* Fine words on paper!

COMFORT: But they mean them. Truly they do.

MILES *(Starting off):* Hurry, Comfort. There's no time. Come. *(MILES and COMFORT exit.)*

HUMPHREY: No doubt I am doing wrong, but I cannot resist the look in their eyes. Why do they, like all the rest, insist on staying in this barren land? Dolts and simpletons, every one. *(Starts to exit, as CAPTAIN JONES enters, followed by GOVERNOR CARVER, ELDER BREWSTER, WILLIAM BRADFORD, JOHN ALDEN, MISTRESS BRADFORD, PRISCILLA MULLENS, MISTRESS HOPKINS, and MEN, WOMEN, and CHILDREN.)*

MASTER JONES: What's that about dolts and simpletons, my lad?

HUMPHREY: 'Tis my opinion, sir, of those who refuse your kind invitation to sail back to England on the *Mayflower.*

MASTER JONES *(Smiling):* An opinion which I share, in part, Master Humphrey, but something tells me these dolts and simpletons are men of great courage and strong faith. *(Points to trunk)* Better get that gear aboard the shallop. We'll be taking off for the *Mayflower* shortly.

MISTRESS HOPKINS *(Coming forward with a parcel and a letter):* Master Jones, pray deliver this letter and parcel for me, when you reach London.

WILLIAM BRADFORD: Enough, Mistress Hopkins. Master Jones is overladen now with our messages and bundles.

MASTER JONES *(Cheerfully):* Always room for one more,

Mistress Hopkins. You may rest assured they will be delivered, have I the good fortune to reach England safely. *(Looks around)* But what about yourselves? Can I not deliver one or two of you as well? *(Laughs)* My offer is still open. I will take anyone who wants to go.

PRISCILLA *(Stepping forward):* Anyone at all, Master Jones?

JOHN ALDEN *(In surprise):* But surely, Priscilla, you would not go back to England, would you?

PRISCILLA *(Wistfully):* I was only thinking of how beautiful England is in the spring, John. The blossoms and the sweet air of spring.

GOVERNOR CARVER: And I have no doubt the thought of home and springtime has made others homesick, too, Mistress Mullens. As Governor of the Colony, I wish to say that anyone who wants to is free to go.

MASTER JONES: In my opinion, it is pure folly for some of you to face another winter here, when you are worn from sickness and lack of proper food.

ELDER BREWSTER: We have endured those hardships, Master Jones, and though we thank you for the offer, we would stay and make the land flourish.

MASTER JONES: But think of the children and the hardships they must endure, if they survive.

WILLIAM BRADFORD: The Chiltons are sending their children back with you, and other parents know they have the same opportunity. *(*MISTRESS *and* MASTER CHILTON *enter.)*

MASTER CHILTON: How long till sailing time, Master Jones?

MASTER JONES: We'll get under way at full tide, sir, almost as soon as we row out to the *Mayflower.* Where are our little passengers?

MASTER CHILTON: That's just the trouble, sir. We don't know.

MISTRESS CHILTON: Has anyone here seen Miles and Comfort? I fear they have wandered off into the forest and are lost.

MASTER CHILTON: Do not fret, Mary. They know every foot of this forest. *(Sternly)* If Master Jones grants me the time, I will fetch them back in time to give them a taste of the birch before they go aboard.

MASTER JONES: Well, sir, we can't delay the sailing. We must catch the tide at its height. If the children are here in time, they are welcome. If not, I'm afraid they will be left behind.

BOY: Miles said he'd never go back to England, no matter what.

GIRL: Hush, Jonathan! Would you be a tell-tale, and get Miles in trouble.

MASTER CHILTON *(Firmly)*: I promise you they will be in bad trouble when I find them. I'm sure they have run away rather than leave Plymouth.

MISTRESS CHILTON *(Tearfully)*: Oh, John, how could they be so disobedient? And what will happen to them in the forest with no food?

HUMPHREY *(Entering)*: The shallop is ready, sir.

MASTER JONES: I am sorry, Master Chilton, but I cannot wait.

MISTRESS CHILTON *(Suddenly)*: The chest! The chest! And the provisions! Where are they?

HUMPHREY: I will unload the chest at once, ma'am. *(Exits)*

MASTER JONES: It is hard for me to bid farewell to such courageous people. I have lived among you for seven months. I have seen you face suffering, starvation, and death without complaint. And now I see you ready to face those same dangers again. It is with real sorrow that I bid you farewell. *(Turns to exit)*

GOVERNOR CARVER: Our thanks and our prayers go with you, Master Jones.

ELDER BREWSTER: May you have a safe journey. *(*SQUANTO *enters, with* COMFORT *and* MILES.*)*

SQUANTO *(Holding his hand up):* Wait! Squanto brings children back for trip on water! *(*COMFORT *runs to parents.* MILES *faces* MASTER CHILTON.*)*

MISTRESS CHILTON: Thank goodness you have come in time.

MASTER CHILTON: Shame on you, Miles! 'Tis your good fortune that I have not the time to give you the trouncing you deserve!

MILES *(Contritely):* I am sorry for running away, Father, and I am glad Squanto made us return.

COMFORT: Squanto says no brave man ever runs from trouble.

SQUANTO: Brave children must learn to face danger. Never run away.

MILES: We thought we were being brave to run away. But now I know we are brave only if we face you and Mother and the rest. *(With resolution)* Father, Comfort and I cannot go with Master Jones on the *Mayflower.*

MASTER CHILTON *(Sternly):* What talk is this? "Cannot go," indeed. You *must* go, because I, your father, *command* you.

MILES *(Unflinchingly):* Nay, Father. You must not force us to go back to England against our will.

MISTRESS CHILTON: Miles! You must not speak so to your father.

MASTER CHILTON: You are but a child. Your parents know what is best for you.

MILES: But we have our rights, sir.

MASTER CHILTON *(Angrily):* Rights? What rights?

MILES: The just and equal laws that Master Bradford wrote about in the Compact you all signed before we left the *Mayflower.*

MASTER CHILTON: I will hear no more of this talk.

GOVERNOR CARVER *(Stepping forward):* Nay, Master Chilton. Let the lad speak. What is this about the Compact, Miles?

MILES: The day we landed, sir. The men all gathered in the cabin of the Mayflower to sign the Compact Master Bradford wrote.

GOVERNOR CARVER *(Listening intently):* Aye, that we did, lad.

MILES: After the gentlemen left, some of us boys went in, and Master Bradford explained the words to us. It said you all agreed to make just and equal laws for the general good of the colony. We asked Master Bradford if those just and equal laws were for everyone, young and old, rich and poor, and he said they were.

MASTER BRADFORD: That is so, Miles. And so they are. The Compact reads that we agree to "enact, constitute and frame such just and equal laws, ordinances, acts, constitutions, and offices, from time to time, as shall be thought most meet and convenient for the general good of the colony."

MILES: And Comfort and I are part of the colony. We have faced the same dangers, we have done our share of the work, and we feel the same strong love in our hearts for this land. Unless it be for "the general good of the colony" to send us away, we claim it is our right to stay here with the rest.

MASTER BRADFORD: Why do you feel so strongly about leaving Plymouth?

MILES: Comfort and I are not too young to remember the talk before we left England. We have not forgotten how our elders spoke of worshiping God without fear in our own way, and told us we would build a strong new colony here in America, where men could work and worship as they pleased. Now we are part of this colony. We want to build it and work with the rest of you.

MISTRESS CHILTON: But think of your future . . . your schooling.

MASTER BRADFORD *(Quietly):* There are scholarly men here, Mistress Chilton. Our children will not grow up in ignorance.

MISTRESS CHILTON: But the dangers . . . the cold, the sickness, the threat of starvation.

SQUANTO: Squanto's friends not starve. Squanto teach you how to plant corn, our way. Good harvest. Plenty for all.

GOVERNOR CARVER: What say you, Master Chilton? Is it for the general good of the Colony that you would have Comfort and Miles sail back to England?

MASTER BRADFORD: Our Colony will need strong young people with clear minds for the work that lies ahead.

MASTER CHILTON *(Looking at wife):* Is it for the general good of the colony, or for the peace of our own minds and hearts, Mary?

MISTRESS CHILTON: Perhaps we have been selfish, John. Let them stay.

MASTER CHILTON: Miles, it looks as if you have won the fight for yourself and Comfort. You shall both stay.

COMFORT *(Happily):* You won't be sorry, Father. Thank you!

MILES: Thank you!

GOVERNOR CARVER: A wise decision, Master Chilton,

and one you will never regret. As for you, Miles and Comfort, remember you promise to obey these same just and equal laws we may henceforth make for the general good of the colony. Do you understand?

MILES: We understand, sir, and we are ready to keep that promise.

MASTER JONES: Well spoken, lad. I am sorry I will not have you and your sister aboard. But good fortune to you both.

MILES: Thank you, sir, and Godspeed! (HUMPHREY *enters, with chest.*)

HUMPHREY: So they caught up with you, did they? Now I'll have to carry this chest down to the boat again.

MASTER JONES: Nay, leave it here, lad. Our passengers are not sailing with us, after all. (*To* GOVERNOR CARTER) Goodbye, sir, and God bless this Colony. (*To* HUMPHREY) Come, we sail at once. (HUMPHREY *and* MASTER JONES *exit. All wave, calling goodbye.*)

PRISCILLA: Oh, John, they're going back home to England.

JOHN ALDEN: This is your home now, Priscilla. Our home, for always. Come, let us all go up to Fort Hill and watch the *Mayflower* sail out of the harbor. (*Curtain*)

THE END

Squeaknibble's Christmas

Characters

MR. GRANDFATHER CLOCK
MOLLY MOUSE
SQUEAKNIBBLE
MAMA MOUSE
MASTER PUSS
FIVE LITTLE MICE

TIME: *Christmas Eve, ten o'clock.*

SETTING: *The Great Hall of a large house. Mr. Grand-father Clock, holding gong, is in one corner. On a low table against the wall there is a small Christmas tree. Chairs stand at both sides of table. Large hammer rests on chair near Mr. Clock. A large sign over center entrance reads* MOUSEHOLE.

AT RISE: MR. GRANDFATHER CLOCK *picks up hammer and slowly strikes ten on his gong.*

MR. CLOCK (*Replacing hammer*): Only ten o'clock. (*Sighs*) Eight more hours to go before the children come to see their tree and open their presents! I get so lonely here. I'd be glad to talk to anyone, even that little Molly Mouse. I wonder where she is tonight. (*Cups ear with hand*) Oh, ho! I think she's coming, and from the amount of noise she's making, she must be in a merry mood! *(MOLLY MOUSE dances in from mousehole, singing.)*

MOLLY MOUSE *(Singing to the tune of "Jingle Bells"):*
>Jingle bells, jingle bells,
>Jingle all the way,
>Oh, what fun it is to skip,
>And scamper all the day!
>Jingle bells, jingle bells,
>Jingle all the way,
>Oh, what fun it is to be
>A mouse on Christmas Day!

(Stops in front of MR. CLOCK)

MR. CLOCK: Well, well, well! You're unusually frisky this evening. Why all the dancing and singing?

MOLLY: Because it's Christmas Eve, that's why. I always feel like dancing on Christmas Eve.

MR. CLOCK: How different you mice are today from the mice we used to have in the good old days! *(Counting on fingers)* Let me see—there was your grandma, Mistress Velvet-paw, and there was Grandfather, Mr. Sniffwhisker! Many a night I've seen them dancing in this old hall, but always the minuet—so elegant and dignified!

MOLLY: Who wants to be dignified on Christmas Eve?

MR. CLOCK: What does Christmas mean to you, Miss Molly Mouse?

MOLLY: It means a great deal to me. It's the night Santa brings me presents because I've been so good. I haven't gnawed any holes, or stolen any canary seed, or worried my mother by running behind the flour barrel where that hateful trap is set. I'm sure Santa Claus will bring me something special tonight.

MR. CLOCK *(Laughing):* Why, you silly mouse! You don't believe in Santa Claus, do you?

MOLLY *(Indignantly):* Of course I do. Didn't he bring me a tasty butter cracker last Christmas, and a crunchy gingersnap and a delicious rind of cheese? I should be very ungrateful if I didn't believe in him! Besides, I'd be afraid not to believe in Santa Claus.

MR. CLOCK: Afraid? Why?

MOLLY: You see, I had a sister named Squeaknibble who didn't believe in Santa Claus, and when I think of what happened to her, a shiver runs straight down my back from my whiskers to the tip of my tail. *(Singing to the tune of "Three Blind Mice")*

>One bad mouse, one bad mouse,
>Lived in a house, lived in a house,
>She had a terrible time because
>She didn't believe in a Santa Claus,
>And you know by now that our tale is about
>That one bad mouse!

MR. CLOCK *(As if thinking aloud):* Squeaknibble! Squeaknibble! That name sounds familiar.

MOLLY: You must remember her.

MR. CLOCK: Let me see. Was she a fat, chunky little mouse with a very pink nose?

MOLLY: No, that's not the one. Squeaknibble was always long and thin. Mother said she took after our New England ancestors. *(Scampers over to* MR. CLOCK *and curls up on floor beside him)* The only trouble with Squeaknibble was that she was such a disbelieving little mouse. I can remember when Mother first tried to tell her about the moon! It was right here in this very hall. *(*MAMA MOUSE *pokes her head out of mousehole. She advances to center. Lights may dim on* MOLLY *and* MR. CLOCK. *A spot shines center on* MAMA.*)*

MAMA: Squeaknibble! Squeaknibble! Come here and look at the beautiful moon.

SQUEAKNIBBLE *(Entering from mousehole):* Where? Where? I don't see any moon.

MAMA *(Pointing):* Way up there above the trees is the moon, sailing back and forth between the clouds.

SQUEAKNIBBLE: Oh, yes. I see it now. What is the moon made of, Mama?

MAMA: As if I haven't told you a thousand times. The moon, my dear little mouse, is made of green cheese.

SQUEAKNIBBLE: Don't be silly, Mama dear. The moon isn't made of green cheese at all! That's just a silly idea for old mice and babies. A really clever mouse wouldn't be fooled for a second.

MAMA *(Angrily):* Squeaknibble, you're much too clever for your own whiskers. One day you'll be a sad mouse, if you don't start believing what we older mice tell you.

SQUEAKNIBBLE *(Impatiently):* I know, Mama, but you always tell such foolish stories! How can you expect me to believe them? It's the same way with Master Puss. You make up such terrible tales about him, I'd be scared out of my skin if I believed half of them.

MAMA *(Warningly):* You'd better believe me, if you expect to stay alive. Master Puss is a monstrous creature, with sharp claws and terrible teeth. You'd never stand a chance if he caught you.

SQUEAKNIBBLE: Don't make me laugh, Mama. Everybody knows a mouse is the fastest thing on four feet. That old Master Puss could never catch me! Do you know what I'd do? I'd go right up and stick my tongue out at him, and I'd say *(Sing-song)* Ny'a, ny'a, ny'a, Master Puss. You can't catch me! *(She sings and cavorts about stage.* MASTER PUSS *enters stealthily behind her, claws outstretched.* SQUEAKNIBBLE *and* MAMA *see him just in time and run into mousehole, squealing.)*

MASTER PUSS *(Stamping his foot):* Aha, little Squeak-nibble! You've escaped me this time, but I'll get you yet. *(Licking his chops)* What a nice, tasty morsel you'll make for my Christmas dinner! *(Thinking aloud)* Let me think. This is Christmas Eve. Maybe that's the very time I can catch you off guard. *(Stalking slowly around stage)* I've been such a good cat this year, I think I'm entitled to Squeaknibble as my Christmas treat. *(He struts about, singing to the tune of "Pussy Cat, Pussy Cat, Where Have You Been?")*

> Pussy Cat, Pussy Cat,
> What is your dream?
> I'd like Squeaknibble all served up in cream!
> Pussy Cat, Pussy Cat,
> What will you do?
> I'll catch Squeaknibble for my Christmas stew!
> Meow! Meow! Meow!

(He hides under table with Christmas tree. Lights come up on MR. CLOCK *and* MOLLY.*)*

MR. CLOCK *(To* MOLLY*):* I do recall your sister, Squeak-nibble. And I remember that particular Master Puss. He was a great, big, black and white fellow, as wily as they come.

MOLLY: That's right! *(With a shiver)* It still gives me a chill when I remember that Christmas Eve. Mama brought us back here to show us the Christmas tree before she put us to bed. Squeaknibble recovered from her fright and was saucier than ever. None of us ever dreamed that Master Puss was under the table. *(Lights dim on* MOLLY *and* MR. CLOCK. *Spotlight goes up on others.* MAMA *sticks her head out of mousehole, enters, then looks cautiously around. She then summons others to enter.)*

MAMA: The coast is clear. You may all come out. *(*FIVE

LITTLE MICE *enter, followed by* SQUEAKNIBBLE.
MAMA *points to tree.)* Isn't it a lovely tree?

ALL *(Ad lib):* Beautiful, just beautiful. How pretty! I
love the star! *(Etc. From time to time during this
scene,* MASTER PUSS *peers out from under table.)*

MAMA: Now that you've all seen the tree, you must be off
to bed. Remember this is the night that Santa Claus
will come.

1ST MOUSE: How will Santa get into our mousehole?

2ND MOUSE: I hope he brings me Roquefort cheese.

3RD MOUSE: I'd rather have Edam cheese. It's milder.

4TH MOUSE: I'd love some good old English cheddar.

5TH MOUSE: Muenster for me.

SQUEAKNIBBLE: How silly you all are with your talk
about Santa Claus.

3RD MOUSE: It's not silly. Santa's really coming tonight.
Mama said so.

SQUEAKNIBBLE: I don't believe it! *(Sticks her tongue
out)* So there.

2ND MOUSE: If you'd hurry and come to bed, he'd be
here in no time.

SQUEAKNIBBLE: I have news for you. I'm not going to
bed at all!

2ND MOUSE: Where are you going?

3RD MOUSE: Santa won't be able to find you when he
comes.

SQUEAKNIBBLE *(Tossing her head):* I don't care anything about old Santa Claus. I'm going to have a good
romp here in the hall, all by myself.

MAMA: You're going to do nothing of the sort. You're
going to bed with the others. Now, all of you into the
mousehole—hurry! *(All exit, except* SQUEAKNIBBLE.*)*
Squeaknibble, run along with the rest, if you know
what's good for you. (MAMA *gives* SQUEAKNIBBLE *a*

shove into mousehole, and exits after her. MASTER PUSS *comes out from under table.)*

MASTER PUSS: Meow! Meow! Meow! Something tells me Squeaknibble will be back here as soon as her mother's back is turned. Now let me see. How can I fool her? She says she doesn't believe in Santa Claus. Hm-m-m. That gives me an idea. I think I saw a fur coat and cap in the closet. They would give me the perfect disguise. I'll give that Squeaknibble the shock of her life. *(MASTER PUSS exits, as* SQUEAKNIBBLE *enters from mousehole.)*

SQUEAKNIBBLE *(Prancing around):* How good it is to get out of that mousehole and frolic here by myself. My stupid brothers and sisters are probably dreaming about Santa Claus this very minute. But not me! And if I see that old Master Puss again, I'll just say, Ny'a, ny'a, ny'a, Mister Pussy Cat can't catch me. *(MASTER PUSS re-enters, in fur coat and cap.)*

MASTER PUSS *(Imitating Santa's voice):* Ho, ho, ho, little mouse! What are you doing up so late on Christmas Eve?

SQUEAKNIBBLE *(Terrified):* Please, please, whoever you are, go away! Please, please, don't hurt me. I'm only a little mouse.

MASTER PUSS: Ho, ho, ho! I would never hurt a good little mouse like you! Don't you know me? *(In a false, sweet voice)* I'm Santa Claus, and I've brought you a tasty piece of nice, fresh cheese.

SQUEAKNIBBLE *(Approaching* MASTER PUSS*):* How nice of you! I never believed there was a Santa Claus, but now—*(*MASTER PUSS *leaps at her with a terrible yowl. After a wild chase around stage, he trips over his coat, and falls, just in time for* SQUEAKNIBBLE *to escape into mousehole.)*

MASTER PUSS (*Shaking his paw as if it were a fist*): I'll get you yet, Squeaknibble. I'll get you yet! (*Spotlight off; lights up full*)

MOLLY: After that, my sister Squeaknibble was a changed character. She went to live with my aunt, who was a country mouse, but when she came back to visit, she would tell us the story over and over again. (SQUEAKNIBBLE *enters with* FIVE LITTLE MICE.)

SQUEAKNIBBLE: Believe me, children, it pays to believe in Santa Claus. I never heard of a child or a mouse who doubted him who came to any good. And remember, I know from experience.

ALL (*Singing to the tune of "Up on the House Top"*):
Squeaknibble taught us the Christmas laws,
We all believe in old Santa Claus.
Into our mousehole we know he'll squeeze,
Just to deliver our Christmas cheese.
Ho, ho, ho, all of us know, ho, ho, ho, all of us know,
Santa will bring us something nice,
If we are good little Christmas mice! (*Curtain*)

THE END

The Christmas Umbrella

Characters

JINGLE ⎫
TINSEL ⎭ *Santa's elves*
MRS. SANTA CLAUS
SANTA CLAUS
GRANDMA UMBERTO
MAMA UMBERTO
THERESA ⎫
CARLOS ⎪
JOE ⎪
STEVE ⎪
BETTINA ⎬ *the nine Umbertos*
ROSA ⎪
MARIA ⎪
JOHNNY ⎪
NICK ⎭
EIGHT NEIGHBORS

SCENE 1

TIME: *Christmas Eve.*
SETTING: *Santa's workshop. The shelves are empty except for one big box and a few scattered toys.*

AT RISE: MRS. SANTA CLAUS *is sitting in a rocking chair, taking a nap. Her glasses have fallen down on her nose.* JINGLE *and* TINSEL *are sitting at table.* JINGLE *is working on a crossword puzzle.*

JINGLE: What is a four-letter word beginning with Y that means Christmas?

TINSEL: That's easy. *Yule. (Spells)* Y-u-l-e.

JINGLE: That's right. *(Prints slowly)* Y-u-l-e. Now, let me see. Where am I? Oh, yes! 23 down. "A spicy holiday drink." What in the world could that be? Seven letters. The third letter could be an S or maybe an X.

TINSEL: I think it's S. Try *wassail.*

JINGLE: How do you spell it?

TINSEL: W-a-s-s-a-i-l. Haven't you ever heard of a wassail bowl?

JINGLE: No. What does a wassail bowl have to do with Christmas?

TINSEL *(Airily):* For a Christmas elf working for Santa Claus, you certainly don't know very much about Christmas customs. A wassail bowl holds the wassail that people drink on Christmas.

JINGLE *(Admiringly):* You're smart, Tinsel. Maybe you should do this puzzle instead of me.

TINSEL: I don't feel like doing puzzles. I'm worried about Santa.

JINGLE: Why?

TINSEL *(Worriedly):* He should be home by now. Maybe something happened to him.

JINGLE: Like what?

TINSEL: Maybe he got tangled up in a TV antenna.

JINGLE: Not a good driver like Santa.

TINSEL: Well, I'm going to look for him. (TINSEL *exits.* MRS. SANTA *wakes with a start.)*

MRS. SANTA: Santa?

JINGLE: No, Mrs. Santa. He's a little late. Tinsel just went to look for the reindeer and the sleigh.

MRS. SANTA: It must be almost dawn. *(Gets up and goes to fireplace, hangs kettle on hook)* I'd better put the kettle on, so Santa can have a good hot drink when he comes in. *(Sound of bells is heard offstage.)*

SANTA *(From off):* Whoa, reindeer!

JINGLE *(Excitedly):* He's coming! I'll go help Tinsel unharness the reindeer. *(Exits)*

MRS. SANTA: I'll pour his cup of tea. *(Pours tea and sets cup on table.* SANTA *enters, pulling off gloves and rubbing hands together.)*

SANTA: Merry Christmas, my dear! It's good to be home again. *(Sits at table)*

MRS. SANTA: Sit right down and have a good, hot cup of tea. You must be frozen.

SANTA: Nonsense! You know I never get cold on Christmas Eve. But a cup of tea will taste good, all the same.

MRS. SANTA *(Taking plate of cookies from sideboard):* And here are some cookies. *(Sets plate on table)*

SANTA: Snickerdoodles! My favorites! *(Takes cookie from plate)*

MRS. SANTA: You deserve the best after your long trip, Santa. How did things go?

SANTA: The trip was more wonderful than ever this year, Mrs. Santa. So many good boys and girls in the world—it just amazes me! *(Chuckling)* And they'll all be happy Christmas morning when they see what I've brought them. By the way, were there any calls?

MRS. SANTA: Just a message about a Christmas tree shortage someplace or other. But the connection was so bad I couldn't make it out.

SANTA: Oh, well. I'm sure it's not serious. *(*JINGLE *and* TINSEL *enter.)*

TINSEL: Did you have a good trip, Santa?

SANTA: Marvelous! *(Looks around with satisfaction)* I don't believe I've ever seen the workshop so cleaned out. You've done a fine job.

JINGLE: I hope we don't get any last-minute requests.

SANTA: I'm sure we won't now. It's almost Christmas morning. *(Points to big box on shelf)* By the way, Jingle, what's in that big box?

JINGLE: Oh, that's just an extra box of umbrellas. Hardly anyone wanted an umbrella this year.

TINSEL: That's not a box of umbrellas, Jingle. That's a box of toys!

JINGLE: No, you're wrong, Tinsel. Those are the umbrellas. I packed them away for next year.

TINSEL: But I looked inside that box after Santa left. It's a box of toys. A pair of roller skates, a baseball glove, three dolls, a toy train, a small radio, a paint set, a chemistry set, and crayons.

SANTA *(Puzzled):* It's mighty strange that all these toys were left over. *(*MRS. SANTA *goes to shelf and inspects box.)*

MRS. SANTA: Here's a label. *(Adjusts her glasses and peers intently at label)* It says, "The Nine . . . The Nine Umbertos." *(Looks up)* What does that mean?

JINGLE: Those are the nine Umberto children. They live at 217 Mason Street in Brookville.

SANTA: 217 Mason Street, Brookville—why, that's where I took the box of nine umbrellas! Goodness! I must have read the label wrong.

MRS. SANTA: I've told you, Santa, you must have your glasses changed.

SANTA: Dear me! The "Nine Umbertos" looked like "Nine Umbrellas" to me, so I delivered the umbrellas to that address.

JINGLE: Oh, Santa! Those children are going to be so disappointed to find umbrellas instead of toys.

SANTA: Disappointed! *(Huffily)* I've never disappointed a single child in my long and honorable career.

MRS. SANTA: Of course, you haven't, my dear! *(To JIN-GLE)* Jingle, what a ridiculous thing to say!

JINGLE *(Insistently):* It isn't a bit ridiculous. Imagine those poor little Umbertos on Christmas morning with no toys.

TINSEL: Jingle is right. They'll be so upset!

SANTA: So! You've lost your faith in your old Santa Claus. *(Sadly)* I might just as well retire!

JINGLE: Now, don't get so upset, Santa. It may not be too late to correct your error.

SANTA *(Angrily):* Stop talking to me about my error! There has been no error! You don't seem to understand that by the time the Umberto children get the umbrellas, they will no longer want the toys they asked for. They'll be tickled pink with the umbrellas! *(JINGLE and TINSEL look at each other and shrug.)* You find that hard to believe, don't you?

JINGLE and TINSEL *(Nodding their heads):* Very, very hard.

SANTA: Then listen to me, and I'll tell you a Christmas secret. When you give a Christmas present with real love, there can be no errors. Those umbrellas were packed in a box that was full of love. The little Umbertos are bound to be happy with them. *(JINGLE and TINSEL shake their heads again. SANTA rises, exasperated.)* Very well, then. Jingle, go harness the reindeer. Tinsel, take this box to the sleigh.

JINGLE: Hurray! You're going to take the toys to the Umbertos after all!

SANTA: No, *you're* going to take the toys to the Umbertos. When you get to their house, leave the toys in the sleigh until you see how the children react when they open the box of umbrellas. If they're unhappy or disappointed, you may deliver the toys. But if they're happy with the umbrellas, bring the toys back.

TINSEL: O.K., Santa. *(Happily)* I couldn't have enjoyed a bite of my Christmas dinner, worrying about those Umberto children.

JINGLE: Bring the box, Tinsel. I'll have the reindeer ready in a jiffy. *(Exits)*

TINSEL *(Picking up box):* Thanks, Santa.

MRS. SANTA *(Handing* TINSEL *two tinsel-printed signs reading,* INVISIBLE*):* Here—don't forget to wear these signs when you go inside the Umberto house. Goodbye, and good luck!

SANTA: Drive carefully, and watch out for those TV antennas! *(*TINSEL *exits. Curtain)*

* * * * *

SCENE 2

TIME: *Several hours later.*

SETTING: *The Umberto living room.*

AT RISE: GRANDMA, MAMA, THERESA, *and* CARLOS UMBERTO *sit in chairs and sofa.*

THERESA: Where's Papa? It's almost daylight.

MAMA: Your papa has his mind made up to find Christmas trees tonight.

CARLOS: But by now he must know that no shipments will arrive in time.

MAMA: Papa does not give up easily. For years this

neighborhood has counted on Papa Umberto for Christmas trees.

GRANDMA *(Sniffing in disdain):* Christmas trees! In Italy we have the *Ceppo*—the Christmas Log.

MAMA: I know, but even in Italy now they have Christmas trees.

THERESA: Poor Papa! He'll be so disappointed.

MAMA: He'll be disappointed for you, too, children. Without the Christmas tree business this year, you won't have as many presents as last year.

THERESA: Don't worry, Mama. This year the presents are taken care of.

MAMA *(Surprised):* What do you mean, Theresa?

THERESA: Early in the month, Carlos and I helped the little ones write to Santa Claus.

CARLOS: They asked for everything they wanted.

THERESA: I even asked for something, too! *(*TINSEL *and* JINGLE, *wearing* "INVISIBLE" *signs, enter and stand at right. They sit.)*

MAMA: Theresa, do you believe in Santa Claus?

THERESA *(Sadly):* When I was writing the letters, I believed. Now I'm not so sure. *(Sound of door opening is heard.)*

MAMA *(Excitedly):* That must be your father! *(*PAPA UMBERTO *enters, carrying large box.)* Tony, you're back!

PAPA: Hello, everyone!

THERESA: We've been waiting for you, Papa.

CARLOS: Did the trees come? Did you find any?

PAPA *(Putting box on floor and sitting):* Not a one! Not a single one! *(Buries head in his hands)* Not only will our own Christmas be ruined, but that of so many others, as well. I have failed them.

MAMA: Nonsense, Tony. Everyone knows you did your best to find trees.

CARLOS: What's in the box, Papa? *(TINSEL and JULIE listen intently.)*

PAPA *(Distractedly):* I don't know. I found it by the chimney in the kitchen.

THERESA *(Excitedly):* It's from Santa Claus. I know it!

PAPA: What is this foolishness?

THERESA: It is not foolish, Papa. Carlos and I wrote letters to Santa Claus for gifts—roller skates for Joe, a baseball glove for Steve, a paint set for Johnny, a train for Nick, dolls for Bettina, Rosa, and Maria, and a chemistry set for Carlos. I asked for a little radio so Mama and Grandma can listen to music all day long.

CARLOS: Let's open the box, Papa! *(PAPA opens box. TINSEL and JINGLE rise.)*

THERESA: Be careful, Papa. You might break something.

MAMA: What's inside? *(PAPA holds up an umbrella.)*

ALL *(Surprised):* An umbrella!

THERESA: Look again, Papa. The toys must be underneath. *(PAPA pulls out eight more umbrellas.)*

CARLOS *(Disappointed):* Nothing but umbrellas!

THERESA: But no one asked for an umbrella.

MAMA *(Musing):* But they are beautiful umbrellas.

GRANDMA: Bah! When it rains, I wear a shawl over my head!

PAPA *(Bewildered):* They are fine umbrellas, and so many of them! I wonder who could have sent them.

MAMA: Maybe they came to the wrong house.

THERESA: No. *(Looks at label)* The label says . . . The Nine Umbrellas!

CARLOS: That's supposed to be *Umbertos*, not *umbrellas!*

THERESA *(Stubbornly):* Then they can't be from Santa Claus. He would never have made such a mistake. *(*TINSEL *and* JINGLE *shake heads.)* I'm so upset, I could cry.

PAPA: Now, now. Listen to me. At least umbrellas are useful. Beside, they're presents. You don't cry over presents.

THERESA: Well, I could cry over these. They're not the presents the children asked for, and they've been so good this year! They were sure Santa would come! *(*TINSEL *and* JINGLE *start to exit, slowly.)*

GRANDMA: In Italy, everything is better. *(Reminiscing; to* MAMA*)* Do you remember the handsome Christmas log your father used to make, with layer after layer of decorations built on a frame above the log?

MAMA: I remember. It looked like a big, golden triangle, with all the sparking ornaments. *(Suddenly)* Say, I know what we can do with the umbrellas! (TINSEL *and* JINGLE *turn to watch, puzzled.)*

CARLOS: What do we need them for? It's not raining.

MAMA: Hush, Carlos. You have heard Grandma tell of the *Ceppo* in Italy, which is decorated and trimmed with Christmas ornaments. In other countries people decorate a sheaf of wheat, or make paper Christmas lanterns.

THERESA: In Mexico they have a *Pinata* . . . a great paper lantern filled with presents.

MAMA: So why not the umbrellas? We'll decorate them as if they're Christmas trees.

ALL *(Astonished):* What?

MAMA: Come on into the kitchen, everyone. I'll show you. *(Grabs a few umbrellas)* Carlos, run upstairs and get the Christmas ornaments from the chest. (TINSEL *and* JINGLE *move center as* CARLOS *exits left.* MAMA,

GRANDMA, PAPA *and* THERESA *exit right.)*

JINGLE: Shall we go get the toys from the sleigh?

TINSEL: Not yet. We'll wait and see what happens.

JINGLE: Do you think Santa may be right, after all?

TINSEL: It's possible. We may have been wrong in doubting him. *(Suddenly, looking off left)* Here comes Carlos. *(*CARLOS *enters with trimmings.* JINGLE *and* TINSEL *return to positions at side.)*

CARLOS: Here are the trimmings. All the tinsel and ornaments, and strings of lights. *(*MAMA *enters, followed by others. She carries an open umbrella. The ribs are wound with tinsel. She put the umbrella on the table, in a little stand.)*

MAMA *(Proudly):* Now for the trimmings. Papa, you arrange the lights. *(Quickly,* UMBERTOS *trim umbrella with Christmas lights, ornaments, tinsel.)*

THERESA: Hand me another red Christmas ball, Carlos. *(He does.)* Now a blue one. *(He does.)*

GRANDMA: Let me put on the icicles.

MAMA *(Pleased):* It's beautiful!

PAPA: Yes, Angela, it really is.

THERESA: This is such fun! I never thought an umbrella could be so wonderful.

MAMA: Don't forget the star! *(*PAPA *puts star on top, then turns on lights.)*

ALL *(Ad lib):* Ah! Wonderful! Almost as good as a real tree! *(Etc.)*

THERESA: I can hardly wait for the little ones to see! *(There is knock at door.)*

PAPA: Visitors, at this hour? *(Exits)*

MAMA: Now, who could that be?

PAPA *(From offstage):* Come in, everyone! Merry Christmas! *(Re-enters, followed by* EIGHT NEIGHBORS*)*

1ST NEIGHBOR: We saw you come home, Tony. Did you get the trees?

2ND NEIGHBOR: I told the children you wouldn't let us down. (PAPA *shakes his head.*)

3RD NEIGHBOR *(Noticing umbrella):* What's this?

PAPA *(Brightening):* It's our Umbrella Tree. Angela and the children made it up.

NEIGHBORS *(Ad lib):* How beautiful! Lovely! *(Etc.)*

4TH NEIGHBOR: But it's an umbrella.

5TH NEIGHBOR: An ordinary umbrella.

MAMA: Not just an ordinary umbrella. This is a Christmas umbrella. It's our Christmas tree.

6TH NEIGHBOR: But umbrellas are expensive. We have none to spare.

7TH NEIGHBOR: Tony, do you have another umbrella like this one?

8TH NEIGHBOR: My children would love this!

PAPA *(Proudly):* Yes, yes! You shall have your Christmas umbrellas, if not your Christmas trees. Carlos, bring in the rest of the umbrellas. (CARLOS *exits right, re-enters carrying umbrellas.)*

1ST NEIGHBOR *(Reaching into pocket):* How much do we owe you, Tony?

PAPA: Not a cent. These umbrellas were gifts to us, and gifts they shall be to our neighbors. (CARLOS *hands out umbrellas.)*

2ND NEIGHBOR: But we must pay you something. The winter has been a hard one. How about some toys for your children? My own have grown too old for some of theirs. Sandra has a beautiful big doll she no longer plays with.

THERESA: Please, Papa! Rosa would love a doll!

3RD NEIGHBOR: We have dolls for your other girls, too, Tony.

1ST NEIGHBOR: I have a paint set, just right for a little boy like Johnny.

5TH NEIGHBOR: My children no longer play with their train set. Would Nick like that?

6TH NEIGHBOR: I'll bet Carlos would like Albert's old chemistry set.

4TH NEIGHBOR: I'm sure Carlos would love that.

7TH NEIGHBOR: My baseball glove would be just right for Steve.

8TH NEIGHBOR: And I've heard Joe asking for roller skates. Let me give you a pair in exchange for the umbrella.

PAPA and MAMA *(Ad lib):* You are all so kind. Thank you. *(Etc.)*

NEIGHBORS *(Ad lib):* Thank *you!* You've saved our Christmas with your umbrellas. Merry Christmas! *(They exit, carrying umbrellas.)*

THERESA: Isn't it wonderful? It's just like a fairy story!

CARLOS: The children will have their tree.

THERESA: And their presents, too. I can hardly believe it.

PAPA: But what about you, Theresa? Didn't you ask Santa for something?

THERESA: Yes, Papa, but maybe I'm too old to get presents from Santa. He brings them only for little children.

PAPA: You may be right. Santa leaves some things for the papas to bring. Go look on the kitchen table. *(THERESA runs out right, re-enters quickly with small radio.)*

THERESA: Oh, Papa! A radio! Let's hear how it sounds. *(Plugs in radio. "Deck the Halls" is heard. As music plays, BETTINA, ROSA, MARIA, STEVE, JOE, JOHNNY and NICK appear at doorway, left.)*

BETTINA: Is it Christmas yet, Mama?

NICK: Has Santa been here?

MARIA: Did he bring my doll?

ALL *(Ad lib):* Look! The tree! What a beautiful tree! *(All join hands and dance around table, singing "Deck the Halls" as curtains close.* TINSEL *and* JINGLE *stand before curtain and recite.)*

TINSEL: We two are still invisible,

JINGLE: Except to you and you. *(Point)*

TINSEL: And we have surely learned a lot,

JINGLE: At least a thing or two.

TINSEL: We know that Santa can't do wrong,

JINGLE: To any girl or boy,

TINSEL: For every single gift he brings

JINGLE: Is packed with Christmas joy.

TINSEL: So if you get a curious gift,

JINGLE: For instance, an umbrella,

TINSEL: Remember every gift upon the earth

JINGLE: Or from the sky above

TINSEL: Is sure to bring you happiness

JINGLE: If packed with Christmas love. *(They exit.)*

THE END

Softy the Snowman

Characters

SANTA CLAUS
STACY'S TOY BUYER
TOYLAND TOY BUYER
GRIMBLE'S TOY BUYER
BONAMAKER'S TOY BUYER
BELL'S TOY BUYER
SPUNKY, *head of Santa's workshop*
MRS. SANTA
MR. SNOWMAN
MARY ⎤
RUTH ⎬ *committee*
BETTY ⎦
SANTA'S WORKERS, *extras*

TIME: *A few days before Christmas.*
SETTING: *Santa's workshop. Desk and chair are up center. Bell is on desk. Large book is in drawer.*
AT RISE: SANTA CLAUS *sits behind desk, demonstrating a mechanical toy to* STACY'S TOY BUYER, TOYLAND TOY BUYER, GRIMBLE'S TOY BUYER, BONAMAKER'S TOY BUYER, *and* BELL'S TOY BUYER.
SANTA (*As the mechanical toy runs down*): There!

That's how it works. Isn't it something?

STACY'S TOY BUYER *(Halfheartedly):* Well, sir, it's all right.

SANTA *(Indignantly):* All right? Is that all you have to say? Why, it's fabulous! Any child who finds this toy in his stocking on Christmas morning will be thrilled!

TOYLAND TOY BUYER: That all depends.

SANTA: Depends on what?

GRIMBLE'S TOY BUYER: It depends on the age of a child.

SANTA: What do you know about children? You don't even have a beard, and you're trying to tell me what children will and will not like.

BONAMAKER'S TOY BUYER: You don't have to grow a beard to know what children like, Mr. Santa.

SANTA: Then suppose you tell me what's wrong with this toy.

STACY'S TOY BUYER: Well . . . it's fine for older children, but little children won't like it.

SANTA: Nonsense! It's sure to make them laugh.

GRIMBLE'S TOY BUYER: But it isn't cuddly.

BONAMAKER'S TOY BUYER: No little boy or girl will want to take it to bed.

SANTA: Cuddly! Washable! We have hundreds of cuddly, washable toys for small children.

BELL'S TOY BUYER: But the children are tired of stuffed dogs and cats and rabbits and pandas and teddy bears. They want something new.

SANTA: Of course they do, and this is the newest thing on the market. *(Holds up mechanical toy)*

STACY'S TOY BUYER *(Sadly):* It just won't do.

BONAMAKER'S TOY BUYER: Sorry, Santa . . .

GRIMBLE'S TOY BUYER: We'll have to look somewhere else. *(*TOY BUYERS *start to exit.)*

SANTA: Where are you going?

STACY'S TOY BUYER *(Turning):* If you don't value our opinion, we might as well leave.

TOYLAND'S TOY BUYER: After all, we department store buyers see what boys and girls ask for.

BELL'S TOY BUYER: We know what makes a toy popular or unpopular.

SANTA *(Raising hand for silence):* Perhaps you'd better go before I lose my temper.

TOY BUYERS *(Ad lib):* We're sorry. All right. Goodbye. *(They exit.)*

SANTA *(Heatedly):* What do they know? Trying to tell me how to run my workshop! Well, I'll show them. *(Rings bell on desk)* Spunky will have the answers. *(Rings bell again, and* SPUNKY *enters)*

SPUNKY: Yes, Santa?

SANTA: Spunky, have you tallied the Christmas letters for this year?

SPUNKY: Yes, sir. Anything special you'd like to know?

SANTA: From the children between the ages of one and six, how many requests did you find for mechanical toys?

SPUNKY: I don't know the exact figure, Santa, but I'd say about three million.

SANTA: Good. And from children of the same age group, how many requests did you have for *(Clears throat)*— cuddly toys?

SPUNKY: Now, that number I can remember, Santa, because it was the largest single item in the lot. Six million, sir.

SANTA: Six million!

SPUNKY: That's right, sir. The little children always ask for toys they can pat and hug and take to bed at night. And mothers always ask to make them washable.

SANTA *(Shaking his head):* I wouldn't expect that.

Those smart aleck toy buyers were right! This puts me in a pretty kettle of fish.

SPUNKY: Is something troubling you?

SANTA: That's putting it mildly. . . . Spunky, what kind of stuffed, cuddly toys do we have on hand?

SPUNKY: Oh, the usual, sir . . . dogs, rabbits, pandas, teddy bears.

SANTA: Don't we have anything new?

SPUNKY: Not a thing, sir. In fact, I was going to bring it to your attention. The children *love* cuddly toys!

SANTA: Please, Spunky. I hate that word "cuddly."

SPUNKY: Then I won't use it, sir. I'll say "squishy" instead.

SANTA: That's even worse. *(Sighs)* If you mean *cuddly*, I suppose you must say *cuddly*. Those young department store buyers think we must put out a brand-new stuffed toy this year, and I don't know what. We've been making dogs and cats and pandas and teddy bears for so long that I can't think of anything new. Do you have any ideas?

SPUNKY *(Shaking his head sadly):* None at all, sir. In fact, I'm having so much trouble in the workshop now, I don't see how we're going to get everything finished—to say nothing of developing a new product.

SANTA: Trouble in the workshop? What is the matter?

SPUNKY: It's Mr. Snowman! He slows up production at every turn.

SANTA: Oh, dear! What has he done now?

SPUNKY: Yesterday he told all the workers in the paint department to take the afternoon off.

SANTA: How could he do such a thing, right in the midst of our busiest season?

SPUNKY *(Shrugging):* He said the workers needed time to do their Christmas shopping.

SANTA *(Angrily)*: He did, did he? Who is he to give orders around this shop? Spunky, send him to me at once.

SPUNKY: Yes, sir. *(Starts to exit, then turns)* Mrs. Santa would never approve if you fired him.

SANTA: Well, er . . . *(Firmly)* Send him in right away.

SPUNKY: Right away. *(Exits)*

SANTA *(Taking record book out of desk drawer)*: Mrs. Santa thinks Spunky is too hard on Mr. Snowman, but his record is a poor one. *(Reads aloud)* Late every morning last week! Fell asleep on the job twice on Tuesday afternoon. Absent Wednesday! And now this! *(*SNOWMAN *enters. He removes his hat and stands leaning on broom.)* Oh, there you are, Mr. Snowman.

SNOWMAN: Spunky told me you wanted to see me, sir. Isn't my work satisfactory?

SANTA: Satisfactory? *(Waving record book at him)* You call this a satisfactory record? Late every morning last week . . .

SNOWMAN: But I had a good reason. You see, every morning on my way to work I pass Billy Barclay's house. You know little Billy Barclay, don't you?

SANTA: Of course I know him. He just broke his leg, didn't he?

SNOWMAN: Yes, and now he's in a cast. . . . Well, right before the accident, he had built a wonderful snowman. Naturally, by the time Billy came home from the hospital, it was almost all melted and out of shape . . . so I've just been helping his mother fool him a little bit.

SANTA: Fool him? How?

SNOWMAN: Well, Billy loves his snowman so much that every morning as soon as he is awake, his mother pushes his wheelchair to the back window to see it.

SANTA: But I thought you said it melted!

SNOWMAN: It did. But I've been taking its place. I stand in the back yard when Billy looks out the window, and then I hurry to work. Since Billy doesn't wake up until almost nine o'clock, it does make me a little late. But, Santa, it's such a small pleasure for such a good little boy.

SANTA *(Clearing his throat):* Ahem! Very kind of you, Mr. Snowman. Under the circumstances, I guess we'll have to excuse you . . . but what about these other offenses? It seems you fell asleep on the job Tuesday afternoon.

SNOWMAN: I'm sorry about that. But you see, I didn't get much sleep on Monday night.

SANTA: That's a poor excuse. What were you doing?

SNOWMAN: I was porch sitting.

SANTA: Porch sitting?

SNOWMAN: Yes. The Mulligans on Plum Street were giving a big party, and they didn't want to spend any money for decorations. So they invited me to stand on the porch all evening.

SANTA: It wasn't very smart of you to tire yourself out like that.

SNOWMAN: Perhaps not. But the Mulligans are such nice people. I wanted to help them out.

SANTA: And what about Wednesday, the day you were absent?

SNOWMAN: I really didn't want to stay out, Mr. Santa, but I just had to help little Piny.

SANTA: Who on earth is little Piny?

SNOWMAN: Little Piny is the small pine tree on the old Watson farm. Piny is such a little tree, his mother couldn't bear to see him cut down this year. The Christmas tree men were coming on Wednesday, and

Piny and his mother didn't know what to do.

SANTA: How did you help?

SNOWMAN: I went to the farm and stood in front of little Piny so the treecutters couldn't see him. Piny was so grateful.

SANTA: Mr. Snowman, you are too much! You leave your job to protect a baby pine tree and then come back and give the painters a half-holiday.

SNOWMAN: But for a good cause—they have to do their Christmas shopping!

SANTA: But you slowed up production, Mr. Snowman. You're just too softhearted for your own good.

SNOWMAN: That's what my family tells me. In fact, that's why they call me "Softy."

SANTA *(Smiling)*: Softy the Snowman. That's a good name for you. Well, Softy, because I'm softhearted too, I'll give you one more chance. But mind you, the very next time you get into trouble, out you go.

SNOWMAN *(Very upset)*: You mean I'll be fired? Oh, Santa, you couldn't do a thing like that. What would I do? Where would I go? You and Mrs. Santa are the only ones who understand me.

SANTA *(Firmly)*: But can't you understand that our work must be done on time? December 24th is our deadline. We're already behind schedule, and Spunky told me that six million children are expecting new cuddly toys on Christmas morning. We haven't had time to design a new one.

SNOWMAN: Oh, dear! That's dreadful. Hm-m-m. Maybe I could think of something.

SANTA: You just keep your mind on your own job. Now, get back to your work bench before we waste any more time. (MRS. SANTA *enters, carrying white teddy bear.*)

MRS. SANTA *(Upset)*: Santa! Look at this!

SANTA *(Going over to her):* What's the matter, dear? Now, just calm down.

MRS. SANTA: I was just down in the workshop, and found three thousand teddy bears ruined—just ruined!

SANTA *(Standing; excitedly):* What? Who did it?

MRS. SANTA: Spunky says it was Mickey Ryan.

SANTA: Impossible! Mickey is our most careful worker. He never makes mistakes.

MRS. SANTA: But he did this time. He forgot to refill the spray gun with brown paint instead of white, and now we have three thousand white teddy bears.

SANTA: This is terrible! Where is Mickey now?

MRS. SANTA: Spunky's looking for him. I guess Mickey was so terrified when he saw what he'd done that he ran away.

SNOWMAN: Oh, he didn't run away. He went to the dentist. He had such a toothache, it just melted my heart to see him suffer, so I told him to run along to the dentist, and I would work the spray gun. I forgot all about changing the paint.

SANTA: Then it was your fault! I might have known! Well, this is it. You're fired.

MRS. SANTA: Santa, you can't fire Softy. We couldn't get along without him.

SANTA: I could get along very well without him!

MRS. SANTA: Who would sweep the snow off our sidewalk every morning? Who would take extra blankets out to the reindeer in the middle of the night? Who would help you in and out of the chimneys when your rheumatism is bothering you? I'm glad somebody around this place has a soft heart.

SANTA: But he's *too* softhearted.

SNOWMAN *(Sighing):* I just can't seem to help it. Whenever I see someone in trouble, my heart just seems to melt and go all squishy-squashy. *(SPUNKY enters with MARY, RUTH, and BETTY.)*

SPUNKY: Sorry to interrupt at a time like this, sir, but here is the committee from the Children's Hospital. They're here to select this year's toys. *(Looking at white teddy bear)* I see you've found out about Mickey's terrible mistake.

SANTA: It wasn't Mickey's fault at all, Spunky. It was Mr. Snowman's. I'll talk to you about it after the hospital committee members have made their decision. *(To girls)* Have you seen all the toys in the workshop?

GIRLS *(Ad lib)*: Yes, sir. They're nice, but . . . *(Etc.)*

SANTA: Is your list ready?

MARY: We have the list for the older children, Santa. Here it is. *(Hands list to SANTA)*

SANTA: Good for you, Mary. *(Glancing at list)* Very good. I think we can fill this order down to the very last ball and bat.

RUTH: And here is the list for the in-betweeners, Mr. Santa. *(Hands list to SANTA)*

SANTA: Thank you, Ruth. *(Looks at list)* I think you've made some good choices.

BETTY *(Uneasily)*: But we don't know what to do about the little children, Santa. They always want cuddly toys.

SANTA *(Putting hands to head)*: I knew it!

SPUNKY: I showed them all the stuffed animals we had, sir, but they want something new.

BETTY: They're very nice, Santa, but the children want something different.

RUTH: And extra soft and squishy.

MRS. SANTA *(Looking closely at SNOWMAN)*: Did I hear you say "extra soft and squishy?"

RUTH: Yes. The little children like to take their toys to

bed, and the softer they are, the more cuddly, the better they like them.

MRS. SANTA: Santa, did you hear that? The children like soft, cuddly toys.

SANTA *(Impatiently)*: I know, but what can we give them outside of our regular stock?

MRS. SANTA *(Sighing)*: Sometimes I think you can't see any further than the end of your own nose. Now, what is the softest, squishiest thing we have around here?

SANTA *(Puzzled)*: I don't know.

MRS. SANTA: You're looking right at him. *(Points to SNOWMAN)*

SANTA *(In disbelief)*: Mr. Snowman?

MRS. SANTA: Yes, Mr. Snowman.

SANTA: But he isn't a toy.

SNOWMAN *(Wistfully)*: But I'd like to be a toy. Why, I can feel my heart beginning to melt right now at the thought of all those little children.

MRS. SANTA: Look at this teddy bear. *(Holds up white bear)* You think it's ruined because it's white? But look again. *(Holds white bear next to SNOWMAN)* Don't you see any resemblance?

SNOWMAN *(Surprised)*: Why, he looks like me.

MRS. SANTA: Of course he does. *(Takes black paper hat from apron pocket and puts it on teddy bear's head, then pulls out black paper buttons, which she pins on teddy bear)* There's your new cuddly toy! How do you like him? His name is "Softy the Snowman."

GIRLS *(Happily; ad lib)*: Oh, he's wonderful. The children will love him. Softy the Snowman! *(Etc.)*

SANTA *(Inspecting toy)*: Well, Spunky, I believe my troubles are over. *(To MRS. SANTA)* My dear, you have really saved the day.

SNOWMAN: And you've saved me too, Mrs. Santa.

SANTA: Indeed she has, Mr. Snowman. From now on you're going to be our symbol. The department stores will display your picture in all the papers. All over the world little children will love you for your soft heart.

SPUNKY: We'll put you into production at once.

MRS. SANTA: I always have a soft place in my heart for softhearted people.

SANTA: And so do I, even though I don't always show it. Now, Spunky, ring the bell and summon the entire staff. I want them to meet this year's Christmas toy of the year—Softy the Snowman. (SPUNKY *rings bell.* SANTA'S WORKERS *enter and line up on stage.* SPUNKY *proposes three big cheers for* MR. SNOWMAN, *and then all begin to sing Christmas song. Curtain)*

THE END

A February Failure

Characters

ANNOUNCER
MISS MARTIN, *teacher*
HARRY HARDWICK
STUDENTS, *any number*
MARY

SETTING: *Classroom, with rows of desks.*

AT RISE: ANNOUNCER *enters, stands at center.*

ANNOUNCER: Did you ever live through a day when everything went dead wrong? Well, that's the sort of day it was for Harry Hardwick. To begin with, Harry slept through his alarm, and the next thing he knew, his mother was shaking him awake. Poor Harry hurried as fast as he could but the bell had rung ten minutes before he dashed into his classroom. (ANNOUNCER *exits.* MISS MARTIN *and* STUDENTS *enter, take seats. All look up as* HARRY *rushes in.*)

STUDENTS (*In jeering tone*): Sleepyhead! Sleepyhead! Couldn't you get out of bed?

1ST STUDENT: Can't you tell the night from day?

STUDENTS: Sleepyhead! Sleepyhead! (*Sing-song*) Lazy

Harry, will you get, will you get up, will you get up. . . .

MISS MARTIN: That will do, class.

ALL: Hurry up! Hurry up! Take your seat and hurry up!

2ND STUDENT: Sleepyhead is late for school.

MISS MARTIN: Well, Harry! What is your excuse? Did you bring your note?

HARRY: I forgot to bring it, Miss Martin. I was in such a hurry. I'll be sure to bring it tomorrow.

MISS MARTIN *(Sternly):* You must really try to be more punctual. Now take your seat quickly, please, and let me see your Lincoln story.

HARRY: My Lincoln story?

MISS MARTIN *(Impatiently):* Now don't tell me you forgot that, too? You know we're having our Lincoln program today, don't you?

HARRY: Good grief! I forgot it! I did write it last night, but I forgot to bring it!

MISS MARTIN: Then sit right down and get to work on another. We were hoping to be able to use yours in our program, but now you have failed us. *(HARRY sits.)* Mary, read your Lincoln story. *(MARY stands, holds paper and starts to read.)*

MARY *(Reading):* "Abraham Lincoln was born so long ago that all the people who actually knew him are dead. But many of those who did know him wrote down the things they remembered about Lincoln and the stories they had heard. Although we do not know if all of these stories are true, some of them are very amusing. Lincoln was a great one for settling arguments. One time two men were arguing about the proper length of a man's legs. Finally they asked Mr. Lincoln's opinion. He studied the problem and then he said: "Well, it's my opinion that a man's legs should be long enough to reach from his body to the ground."

MISS MARTIN *(Smiling):* Good. That's a popular Lincoln story, Mary, and you've told it very nicely. *(To* HARRY*)* Now, Harry, can you figure out how old Lincoln would be if he were living today?

HARRY *(Writing on piece of paper):* Let's see . . . no, that's not right. *(Crossing out)* I'd better start over again.

MISS MARTIN: You shouldn't have any trouble with that, Harry. It's a simple subtraction problem.

HARRY: You subtract the year in which Lincoln was born from this year, 198-. *(Insert correct year)*

MISS MARTIN: That's exactly right. Now go ahead.

HARRY *(Scratching head):* But that's where I'm stuck. I can't remember the year he was born.

MISS MARTIN *(Impatiently):* We talked about it only yesterday, Harry. Tell him the date, class.

STUDENTS: 1809.

MISS MARTIN: Right. Now, Harry, what's the answer? *(He writes.)*

HARRY: Seventy-seven.

MISS MARTIN: I'm afraid you've made Mr. Lincoln too young. Try again. *(He writes again.)*

HARRY: Oh, I see. He'd be 177 years old. *(Adjust figure to current year)*

MISS MARTIN: That's more like it. Now, everyone write this sentence: "If Lincoln were alive today, he would be one hundred and seventy-seven years old." *(As* HARRY *starts to write)* Harry, how do you spell *Lincoln?*

HARRY: L-i-n-c-o-n.

MISS MARTIN: Can anyone correct that?

3RD STUDENT: He forgot the second "l." L-i-n-c-o-l-n.

MISS MARTIN: I'm afraid Harry is forgetting too many things today. But now it's time to practice our program. Let's try our Lincoln song. (*All except* HARRY *sing a song about Lincoln.*) What's the matter, Harry? You aren't singing.

HARRY: I—I don't feel much like singing, Miss Martin. I—I don't know all of the words.

MISS MARTIN: Then perhaps you'd better study the words so you can sing them this afternoon. Now where are the children for the Lincoln portraits? (FOUR STU- DENTS *rise, walk center, stand in line.* 1ST STUDENT *carries picture of Lincoln.*)

1ST STUDENT: Lincoln was a fine man,
Lean, and tall, and strong.
Lincoln always had a joke,
A laugh to pass along.

2ND STUDENT: Lincoln was a kind man,
Quick to sympathize.
To see a fellow creature hurt
Brought tears into his eyes.

3RD STUDENT: Lincoln was a plain man,
Simple in his taste;
Never was a rich man
With money he could waste.

4TH STUDENT: Lincoln was an honest man,
Always on the square.
Lincoln was a just man,
Believed in playing fair.

(*All but* 1ST STUDENT *return to seats.*)

MISS MARTIN: That's a splendid description of Lincoln. I hope you will always remember what he stood for. Now Harry, please take the picture. (1ST STUDENT *hands picture to* HARRY *as he steps forward.* 1ST STUDENT *returns to seat.*) When you say your poem, Harry, hold the picture as if you're actually talking to it.

HARRY: I don't believe I can say my poem, Miss Martin.

MISS MARTIN: Why not? You knew it perfectly yesterday.

HARRY: I still know it. . . . I just don't think I can say it.

MISS MARTIN: But why not?

HARRY: It's this picture. It's just as if Mr. Lincoln is staring straight at me and sees what a failure I am.

MISS MARTIN *(Kindly):* Why, Harry, what do you mean?

HARRY *(Sadly):* I've failed at everything this morning. I was late. I didn't have my Lincoln story. I couldn't figure out how old Lincoln would be, and I even forgot the words of our song. *(Sighs)* I never do anything right.

MISS MARTIN: I'll admit this has been a bad day for you, Harry, but we all have our failures, you know . . . even Lincoln.

HARRY: Oh, no. Not Lincoln, Miss Martin. You can see just by looking at his picture that he was never a failure.

MISS MARTIN *(Cheerfully):* Perhaps this is the time for me to give you our Lincoln surprise, boys and girls. You know, every year on Lincoln's birthday, I like to give the class a little gift in his memory. Last year it was this picture. This year I've chosen something different. Sit down, Harry, and let me show you. I'll take Lincoln's picture. *(HARRY hands her picture, goes to desk and sits. MISS MARTIN puts picture on her desk, then picks up a package.)* We all know that Abraham Lincoln was born in a log cabin in the wilderness, and that he rose to success and fame through hard work and courage. But I wonder if we know about his failures?

STUDENTS *(Ad lib):* Failures? No. Not Lincoln. *(Etc.)*

MISS MARTIN: Yes, lots of them. This year I didn't know what to bring you on Lincoln's birthday. I first thought of a little statue, another picture, some books about his life. . . . and then I saw this—*(Unwrapping gift)* a framed copy of "Lincoln's Failures." I'd like you to come up here and read it. (SEVEN STUDENTS *stand and go to her desk.)* Each of you can read a line.

1ST STUDENT *(Reading):* When Abraham Lincoln was a young man, he ran for the legislature of Illinois and was badly defeated.

2ND STUDENT *(Reading):* He next entered business, but he failed, and spent the next seventeen years of his life paying off the debts of his partner.

3RD STUDENT *(Reading):* He entered politics but was badly defeated in the election.

4TH STUDENT *(Reading):* Then he tried to get an appointment to the United States Land Office, but he failed.

5TH STUDENT *(Reading):* He became a candidate for the United States Senate and was badly defeated.

6TH STUDENT *(Reading):* In 1856 he became a candidate for the vice-presidency of the United States, and was once again defeated.

7TH STUDENT *(Reading):* In 1858 he was defeated by Stephen Douglas.

MISS MARTIN *(Reading):* But in the face of this defeat and failure, he finally won the greatest success in life, and undying fame. In 1860, he was elected the 16th president of the United States. (STUDENTS *return to seats.)* So, my Lincoln gift this year is a list of Abraham Lincoln's failures. We'll hang this right beside his picture so that when you meet with failure and are discouraged, you can say to yourself: "If he could succeed after all those failures and disappointments, so can I."

HARRY *(Happily):* Thanks a lot, Miss Martin. That's the

best present you could have given us. Could I practice
my poem for the program now?

MISS MARTIN: Certainly, Harry. Stand right here, and
we'll all listen.

HARRY:

When Lincoln saw the stars aglow
In his Kentucky sky,
Did he feel timid and alone,
And just as small as I?

And when he heard the night wind
Come howling at the door,
Did he slide down inside his bed
And shiver at its roar?

And when he had to go alone
For water in the night,
Did he walk a little faster?
Did he feel a tiny fright?

And when he had some work to do—
Hard work instead of play,
Did Lincoln ever put it off
Until another day?

I'd give a lot to know these things,
For though I plainly see
I'll never be like Lincoln,
Perhaps *he* was like me!
(STUDENTS *applaud.*)

MISS MARTIN: Well done, Harry! I think you've learned
a good lesson from Lincoln about handling failure. And
you'll all find the secret of Lincoln's triumph over failure in the verse we learned yesterday. Let's say it
together.

ALL *(Reciting):*
　　I will if I can, and I can if I try.
　　I'll keep right on trying and never say die!
　　And if I meet failure perhaps now and then,
　　I'll never give up, but start over again.
　　(Curtain)

THE END

The Missing Linc

Characters

MISS GRAY, *the librarian*
PEGGY STONE, *Linc's sister*
MR. STONE, *writer and Lincoln scholar*
MARTHA STONE, *Linc's stepmother*
MR. SAWYER
FREDDIE SAWYER, *his son*
LINCOLN STONE, *the missing "Linc"*

TIME: *The present.*
SETTING: *The living room of the Stone family. A sofa is at one side and chairs and tables with lamps are placed around the stage.*
AT RISE: PEGGY *is reading a magazine. Doorbell rings insistently.*
MR. STONE *(Coming to doorway right; irritably):* Can't somebody in this house answer that infernal bell? Martha! Peggy! Where is everyone?
PEGGY: I'll get it, Father. *(Rises and goes to door)*
MR. STONE *(As he exits):* And if it's anyone for me—I'm seeing no one this afternoon. *No one!*
PEGGY: Yes, Father. I understand. *(Opens door)* Miss Gray, I'm so surprised to see you! Please come in.

(PEGGY *moves center, followed by* MISS GRAY, *who carries a messy book.*)

MISS GRAY: Peggy, I've come to see your father.

PEGGY: I'm sorry, Miss Gray, but Father can't see anyone. He's at a difficult place in his book, and he's spending every minute at his typewriter.

MISS GRAY *(Firmly):* I know that your father is a famous Lincoln scholar, but he is also a taxpayer and the father of a seventh-grader, Lincoln Stone, so I must insist upon seeing him.

PEGGY: But you don't understand, Miss Gray. We never disturb Father when he's working.

MISS GRAY: I've come about your brother. *(Holds up book)* Just look at this book. I just want you to see the way your brother returned it to the school library.

PEGGY *(Reading title):* The Almighty Atom, by John O'Neil. *(Looks up)* Linc is always reading books on chemistry and physics. He's very smart for his age.

MISS GRAY *(Tartly):* He might be smart about science, but not when it comes to taking care of books. This isn't the first book he's mistreated.

PEGGY: Well, er—you see, Miss Gray, Linc is a real bookworm. He reads every place and any place he happens to be. . . . He even invented a rack to hold a book so he could read in the bathtub . . . and, well, I guess that book must have slipped into the water.

MISS GRAY: That sounds exactly like him. *Chemistry Today* has a big hole in it where he spilled sulphuric acid, and *The Boy Scientist* is warped because he'd put it on a radiator.

PEGGY *(Quickly):* That was my fault, Miss Gray. I turned on the heat in the room, but didn't see the book. Don't blame Linc for that.

MISS GRAY: I have no patience with people who are

careless with books. *(Emphatically)* None at all!

PEGGY: But Linc isn't careless, he's just unlucky. When he's reading, he forgets about everything.

MISS GRAY: Then he must be taught how to remember. This book is brand new, and it's completely ruined. Your father will have to pay for it.

PEGGY *(Upset):* Miss Gray, you can't tell Father!

MISS GRAY *(Indignantly):* Why not? That's exactly why I came!

PEGGY: But Father is so busy, and . . . well . . . not exactly cross, but edgy because his book isn't going well. And besides, he doesn't understand Linc sometimes. You wouldn't want to see my brother get into trouble, would you?

MISS GRAY *(Softening):* I just want to have this book replaced.

PEGGY: Well, then, couldn't you just let Linc pay for the book himself out of his allowance? He could pay it in installments.

MISS GRAY: He already owes the library four dollars and ninety-two cents that he's paying off in installments. *(Shakes her head)* No, Peggy, I insist on settling this with your father. Linc needs some discipline.

PEGGY: Couldn't you come back some other day when Father isn't quite so upset? You see, he's already cross with Linc for something that happened this morning, and if he hears about the book, I don't know what he'll do.

MISS GRAY: Perhaps he should hear about this book.

PEGGY: But Father may make him drop some of his activities. It would break Linc's heart if he couldn't stay on as President of the chemistry club and the debating team, and he's science editor of the *Banner Weekly.* Please, Miss Gray, don't talk to Father now.

Wait till Martha, our stepmother, comes home. She's good at smoothing things over. I'll pay for the book myself from my allowance.

MISS GRAY *(Smiling):* You are a staunch admirer of your brother, aren't you, Peggy? It's not often that a sister defends her brother so loyally.

PEGGY: It's not often that a sister has a brother like Linc. *(Warmly)* He's wonderful, Miss Gray. Since Mother died, we stick together on everything.

MISS GRAY *(Smiling):* I can see that. For your sake, I won't go to your father this time, but be sure to tell Lincoln for me that he has till the end of next week to pay his library bill in full.

PEGGY *(Happily):* Oh, thanks, Miss Gray! You're great. He'll pay every cent. He has a job after school now.

MISS GRAY: Humph! He'll probably be reading a magazine in the back room when he should be waiting on customers. But you're not to blame for your brother's misdeeds, so I'll be off.

PEGGY: Thanks a million, Miss Gray.

MISS GRAY: Goodbye. *(Exits)*

PEGGY *(Sinking into a chair):* Whew! That was a close call. *(*MR. STONE *enters, polishing his glasses.)*

MR. STONE: Who was at the door?

PEGGY: I'm sorry we disturbed you, Father. It was Miss Gray.

MR. STONE: Miss Gray? I don't know any Miss Gray.

PEGGY: She's our school librarian.

MR. STONE: Is that so? Has that brother of yours come home yet?

PEGGY: Not yet. He's working at the drugstore for Mr. Phipps.

MR. STONE: Oh, yes. I had forgotten. Well, I want to see him the minute he comes in. Don't forget.

PEGGY: Even if you're working?

MR. STONE: Yes.

PEGGY *(Anxiously):* Is anything wrong?

MR. STONE: Is anything wrong? There's always something wrong where Linc's concerned. I met Miss Harmon, his English teacher, downtown, and she showed me his last composition.

PEGGY: Wasn't it all right? Linc does pretty well with compositions.

MR. STONE: Just look at what Linc passed in *(Pulls paper from pocket and hands it to her),* and see what you think.

PEGGY *(Reading):* "An Atomic Headache" . . . *(Looks up)* That's a good title, isn't it?

MR. STONE: I'm not concerned with the title. See what it's written on—the telephone bill!

PEGGY: I remember now! Linc got the idea on the way to school, on the bus. He didn't have any paper, so I gave him that old telephone bill to write on. I had it in my purse. I guess he didn't have time to recopy it.

MR. STONE *(Shaking his head):* Just another example of his carelessness. I don't know what will become of him. Most of the time, he's got his nose in a book, and his head in a cloud.

PEGGY *(Timidly):* But, Father, you like books, too. You even write them.

MR. STONE: It's all right to like books and I'm glad Linc has a brain, but he must learn to pay attention to the practical side of life. Maybe he'll just have to give up some of his extra activities. *(Sighs)* Well, I must get back to the typewriter.

PEGGY: Isn't your book going well?

MR. STONE: It isn't going at all. The last three chapters came back again yesterday. I have to revise them.

PEGGY: Those publishers always liked your work before. Why, you know more about Abraham Lincoln than all the history books put together.

MR. STONE: Maybe I know too many facts. They keep telling me they want more atmosphere, more human interest . . .

PEGGY: It must be terrible to write pages and pages and then write them all over again.

MR. STONE: I've rewritten some chapters four or five times.

PEGGY: Martha says you're just tired from working too hard.

MR. STONE: Oh, Martha babies me almost as much as she babies Linc. *(Doorbell rings.)* Please answer the door, Peggy, and if it's anyone for me. . . . I am "out." *(Starts to exit right, as* PEGGY *starts to door, left. Before either one has taken two steps,* MR. SAWYER *storms in, pushing his son,* FREDDIE, *ahead of him.* FREDDIE's *shirt is torn and dirty, and he has a black eye.)*

MR. SAWYER *(In a rage):* I demand to see Mr. Stone at once!

PEGGY: My father is busy.

MR. SAWYER: Not too busy for my business! *(Catches sight of* MR. STONE*)* Oh, there you are, Mr. Stone.

MR. STONE *(Coldly):* Your business must be very urgent, sir, to burst in this way.

MR. SAWYER *(Loudly):* Urgent is right. I'm Jim Sawyer, and this is my boy, Freddie. I want you to take a good look at him.

PEGGY: He looks as if he's been in a fight.

MR. STONE: And on the losing side, I should say.

MR. SAWYER: Exactly. And the bully who attacked my son is Lincoln.

MR. STONE: Lincoln? Are you sure?

MR. SAWYER: Of course, I'm sure. *(To son)* Freddie, tell Mr. Stone exactly what happened.

FREDDIE *(Sniffling):* I just went into the drugstore after school and some other boys came in, and we got into an argument.

MR. STONE: An argument with my son?

FREDDIE: No. With some other boys, and then, Linc had to butt in. He thinks he owns the place. He started pushing me around and then he slugged me—right in the eye. *(Points to his eye)*

MR. SAWYER: I'll speak to Mr. Phipps. This will cost your son his job.

PEGGY: Excuse me, but who were those other guys? *(To FREDDIE)* Were they Steve Mullins and Lenny Ryan?

FREDDIE *(Defiantly):* So what if they were?

PEGGY: Well, were they?

FREDDIE *(Uneasily):* Yeah. What about it?

PEGGY: Mr. Phipps will want to hear about this. *(To MR. STONE)* Steve and Lenny hang out at the drugstore every day, just to make trouble. And Freddie's always with them.

FREDDIE: I am not.

PEGGY: Yes, you are. You push the little kids around. *(To MR. STONE)* I heard Mr. Phipps tell them the other day he'd throw them out if they started any more trouble. I guess he wasn't there today, so Linc did the job for him.

MR. STONE: Maybe this puts a different light on things, Mr. Sawyer. I'm sure you want to be fair, so why not check with Mr. Phipps? You're welcome to use my phone.

MR. SAWYER: No, I'll see him in person, and if your daughter's story is true, I'll have something to say to you, Freddie Sawyer. (*Glares at* FREDDIE)

FREDDIE: She's just covering for him because she's his sister.

MR. SAWYER: Mr. Phipps isn't his sister. He'll tell the truth. Mr. Stone, please forgive me for blowing up. I'm afraid I was pretty hot under the collar.

MR. STONE: I understand. I'll ask Lincoln about this when he comes home.

MR. SAWYER: Thank you. (*To* FREDDIE) Now come along, and we'll talk to Mr. Phipps. (*He and* FREDDIE *exit.*)

PEGGY: This has been a bad day for Linc.

MR. STONE: Yes, but in this case, I'm inclined to side with Linc.

PEGGY: I'm glad. Those kids are always picking on somebody, and if they picked on Linc, they got the wrong guy.

MR. STONE (*Looking at watch*): I wonder why Linc's so late. It's almost supper time, and Martha isn't home, either. (MARTHA *enters. She wears coat and hat and carries a purse, suit box, and another package.*)

MARTHA: Here I am! Who were those two I passed outside? Friends of ours?

MR. STONE: Not exactly. (*Shakes his head*) Just more complaints about Lincoln. It seems he has now gone in for boxing.

MARTHA (*Smiling*): From the looks of his opponent he must be doing all right.

PEGGY: Have you been shopping?

MARTHA: I have. And I want to show you what I bought. (*Opens suitbox and holds up suit*) A present for Linc.

PEGGY (*Smiling*): He'll love that.

MR. STONE: A new suit for Linc?

MARTHA: He needs one. He ruined his good brown suit

last night when he climbed that telephone pole to get the Jones's kitten.

MR. STONE *(Firmly)*: Martha, you'll have to take that suit back.

MARTHA *(Upset)*: But it's his birthday present. Have you forgotten about his birthday?

MR. STONE: Of course not. But you can't give him a suit. I told him just this morning that he would have to wear that brown suit just as it is. He had no business climbing a telephone pole in his best clothes.

MARTHA: But the Joneses asked him to.

MR. STONE: I'm sorry. I'm not going back on my word.

MARTHA *(Putting suit in box and handing it to* PEGGY*)*: Take this upstairs, Peggy, and put it on my bed. And while you're up there you can wrap up the chemistry book we bought Linc last week.

PEGGY: O.K., Martha. *(Exits)*

MARTHA: Martin, I wish you would try to be more understanding. Linc has his faults, but most of his troubles come from perfectly good motives. *(Phone rings.)*

MR. STONE: I'll get it. *(Picks up phone; speaks into it)* Hello. . . . Yes, Martin Stone speaking. . . . Oh, Mr. Phipps. What can I do for you? . . . . Lincoln? No, he isn't here. . . . We thought he was working late. . . . He left early? . . . We haven't seen him. Yes, I'll call you as soon as he comes in. Is he in any trouble? . . . Oh, the fight. Yes, we heard about it. . . . Did Mr. Sawyer pay you a visit? . . . Well, I'm glad you told him you were pleased. I'll be sure to tell him you said so. Thanks a lot. Goodbye. *(Hangs up receiver)* Now, where could he be? Mr. Phipps said he left the store early. *(Shakes his head)* Late for supper again.

MARTHA: Maybe he's at Jim Blainey's. I'll call and see.

MR. STONE *(Sternly)*: And tell him to come home at

once. He and I have a lot to talk about.

MARTHA *(Dialing phone):* I hope he's there. *(Into phone)* Hello, Jim. . . . This is Mrs. Stone. Is Linc there? . . . He isn't. . . . You saw him where? . . . All right. . . . No, I won't worry. . . . Goodbye. *(Hangs up)* Jim just saw Linc getting on a bus. Do you suppose he's running away?

MR. STONE *(Angrily):* This is the last straw. Positively the last straw. That boy needs some discipline.

MARTHA: Discipline! He needs more than that. He needs understanding, too. *(Shakes head)* Martin, your publishers were right. You just don't understand boys.

MR. STONE *(Annoyed):* What do my publishers have to do with this?

MARTHA: Plenty. *(Hands him package and envelope)* Here are more chapters of your book back for revision. And here is a letter. Read it.

MR. STONE *(Reading):* "Dear Mr. Stone: Your *Boy's Life of Abraham Lincoln* is another example of your fine scholarly writing, but it lacks the insight and understanding of boyhood necessary to appeal to young readers. We suggest you retell the story from the viewpoint of an adolescent boy, injecting more human interest and a more sympathetic attitude toward the boy's problems."

MARTHA: Don't you see, Martin, you can't show Abraham Lincoln as a real live boy because you don't understand what makes a real boy tick. If you don't understand your own son, how could you understand that other boy who lived so long ago? After all, boys are boys, whether they're making history or just making trouble.

MR. STONE *(Sighing):* Maybe you're right, Martha. Maybe I'm a failure as a writer and as a father.

MARTHA: Nonsense! You just have the wrong slant. Try to understand Linc a little better, and you'll get closer to the other Lincoln, too. Just pretend you're writing about Linc instead of Abe Lincoln.

MR. STONE: I must say, I fail to see any similarity between them.

MARTHA: You're so busy making Abraham Lincoln a great person that you forget he was ever just a boy.

MR. STONE: You act as if I don't love Linc just because I can't see any signs of greatness in him.

MARTHA: That's just because you are his father. I'll bet Thomas Lincoln was disgusted with his overgrown son many times. *(Reading from manuscript)* Take this, for example. "The boy Lincoln was hungry for books. Upon one occasion when rain came in at the chinks of the loft where he slept, and ruined a book he had borrowed from a neighbor, he pulled fodder for two days to pay for it." That sounds very noble in a book, doesn't it? But I'll bet his dad felt just the way you do when our Linc has an accident with a book or has to pay a library fine.

MR. STONE *(Smiling)*: You should have been a lawyer. Perhaps I should write a note to Linc's English teacher reminding her that President Lincoln scribbled the Gettysburg address on a torn scrap of wrapping paper. Linc wrote his composition on the back of the telephone bill.

MARTHA: The comparison isn't as farfetched as you think. In books, that's the way heroes are made, but in real life that's the way a boy gets into trouble.

MR. STONE: I see your point, Martha.

MARTHA *(Firmly)*: And this new suit business is just one more point. Your books tells how Lincoln dismounted from his horse and waded through mud to rescue a little pig that was stuck under a rail fence. How do you suppose his clothes looked after that good deed?

MR. STONE (*Smiling*): Yes, Martha. I guess I've been expecting Linc to be a model boy, and I've made Abe Lincoln in the book too much of a model to be human. Maybe that's my trouble as a father and as a historian. (*Calling*) Peggy . . .

PEGGY (*Offstage*): Yes, Father. (PEGGY *appears at door right.*)

MR. STONE: Will you bring that new suit down?

PEGGY: Sure. (*Exits*)

MARTHA: Oh, Martin . . . I'm so worried about Linc. Suppose he's run off? Do you think we should call the police?

MR. STONE: Now who's talking nonsense? I might be a washout in some respects, but I have enough confidence in Linc to know that he is not a runaway.

PEGGY (*Entering with suitbox*): Here's the suit. (*Puts box on table*)

MR. STONE (*Reaching into his pocket*): Just open it and take out the trousers. I have a contribution for Linc's pocket. (*Hands her a ten-dollar bill*) The pockets of a new suit should never be empty. Here's a ten spot to wish him a happy birthday.

PEGGY (*Happily*): You are generous, Dad!

MARTHA: Take the suitbox upstairs, Peggy, and wrap it up. Hurry . . . (*As* PEGGY *starts to exit,* LINC *enters. They nearly collide.*)

LINC: Hey, there!

PEGGY (*Flustered*): Oh, dear, Linc. Let me go . . . I have to wrap this.

LINC: What's that? (*Teasing*) A birthday present?

MARTHA: Right. Linc's caught us in the act, Peggy, but

go wrap it up anyway, and he can open it at the dinner table. (PEGGY *exits.*)

MR. STONE: If we ever get to the dinner table. Which reminds me, Linc. Where have you been? We've been worried sick.

MARTHA: Jim Blainey said he saw you get on a bus.

LINC: Yes, I had to ride out to Glendale.

MR. STONE: What was going on in Glendale?

LINC (*Embarrassed*): Well, Dad, you always catch me in my dumb mistakes. You see . . . Mrs. Atkins came in for some film, and I gave her the wrong kind. As soon as she left, I realized I had given her the wrong kind, so I went out to her house to exchange the rolls.

MARTHA: Did you really go all the way out to Glendale for a roll of film?

LINC: Sure. It was my mistake, and I knew the film I gave her wouldn't work in her camera.

MARTHA: But couldn't you have mailed it to her, or exchanged it later?

MR. STONE (*Laughing*): You forget, Martha, that boys named Lincoln take their responsibilities as storekeepers too seriously to let dinner or distance interfere with duty. Let's see, now. . . . How far did the storekeeper, Abe Lincoln, walk to return a penny change to a customer?

MARTHA: You're making fun of me, Martin.

MR. STONE: I'm only proving that for once I do understand. (*Laughs*)

LINC: I was afraid you might be angry because I'm so late. Is your book going better?

MR. STONE: It will, Linc, it will—with your help.

LINC: With my help! Gosh, Dad, history isn't my line. Now if it was chemistry . . .

MR. STONE: It is chemistry, in a way. I want you to teach

me the formula for a real live American boy and what
makes him tick.

PEGGY *(Entering):* I'm hungry. When do we eat?

MARTHA: As soon as you set the table, and I broil the
chops.

MR. STONE: Sooner than that. Just as soon as we can
jump in the car and drive down to the Mayflower Inn.
We're dining out tonight in honor of Linc's birthday.

PEGGY: Great!

LINC: Thanks a lot, Dad.

MR. STONE: And after dinner, how about going bowling
with me, Linc? Peggy and Martha can go to a movie.

LINC: O.K., Dad.

MARTHA: But, Martin, don't you want to work on your
book this evening?

MR. STONE: I'll be working on it every minute. I'll be
getting better acquainted with my hero. *(Slaps* LINC
on the back) Get your hats and coats, everyone. I'm
starved! *(Quick curtain)*

THE END

The Tree of Hearts

Characters

KING VALENTINO, *of Valentia*
PRINCE VALENTINO, *his son*
LORD CHANCELLOR
MR. GOOSEBERRY, *head gardener*
MRS. GOOSEBERRY, *his wife*
GOLDIE GOOSEBERRY, *their daughter*
DALE DAWSON, *American tourist*
GAIL DAWSON, *his sister*
CHILDREN, *extras*

SCENE 1

SETTING: *The Palace Garden of Valentia, near the Head Gardener's hut. Painted backdrop of flower beds and Mr. Gooseberry's trees may be used.*

AT RISE: KING VALENTINO *is talking to* MR. GOOSEBERRY. LORD CHANCELLOR *is taking notes.*

KING: Those are my orders, Mr. Gooseberry. Are there any questions?

MR. GOOSEBERRY: If Your Majesty could just give me some clue as to the type of tree His Highness, the Prince, would prefer?

KING: That is *your* problem, Mr. Gooseberry. My Lord Chancellor has set forth the specifications. Read the order, Lord Chancellor.

LORD CHANCELLOR *(Reading from scroll):* "As King of Valentia, I hereby decree that our Royal Head Gardener develop a special tree for His Highness, the Prince of Valentia, for the occasion of the Prince's tenth birthday, to be celebrated on February 14th. Said tree must possess such charm and power to attract the Prince to the Palace Garden and revive his pleasure therein. Failure to produce such a tree by the date specified will result in the banishment of the Gardener and the Gardener's family from this realm forever. Signed . . . His Mighty Majesty, King Valentino of Valentia."

MR. GOOSEBERRY *(Protesting):* But, Your Majesty, it is impossible to create a new tree by February 14th. That is the day after tomorrow.

KING: You have heard the royal command. I need hardly explain how important it is to lure the Prince back into the garden. It was once his favorite spot. Now he spends all of his time indoors, shut up in his room. He is growing thin and pale. As the Head Gardener, you must make the garden such a beautiful place that he will want to spend hours out here in the sunshine. You have developed many wonderful trees in the past which have delighted the Prince. Surely your skill has not failed you. Come, Lord Chancellor, we have other business to transact. Mr. Gooseberry, we will await a report. (LORD CHANCELLOR *steps in front of* KING *and leads way as they exit.)*

LORD CHANCELLOR: Make way! Make way for His Most Gracious Majesty, King Valentino of Valentia. *(*KING *and* LORD CHANCELLOR *exit.)*

MR. GOOSEBERRY *(Sitting on bench; despairingly):* Alas! Alas! What is to become of us? Where will we go? I have lived all my life in Valentia. I cannot bear to live anywhere else. *(*MRS. GOOSEBERRY *enters, carrying small basket.* GOLDIE, *carrying large straw hat, follows.)*

GOLDIE: Look, look, Father! See what I've brought you from the market. *(Places hat on* MR. GOOSEBERRY's *head)* There's a brim large enough to keep the sun off your head even on the hottest days.

MRS. GOOSEBERRY: We don't want you having a sunstroke working with your flower beds in this hot sun. *(Sighing)* I wonder how it must be living in a country where the summer lasts only a few months of the year.

MR. GOOSEBERRY *(Sadly):* You may soon discover what it is like to live in a different country.

MRS. GOOSEBERRY *(Alarmed):* What do you mean?

GOLDIE: Father, you look so sad. What is the matter?

MR. GOOSEBERRY: A terrible trouble has befallen us. The King was just here.

GOLDIE: The King? That old monster! He always brings trouble.

MR. GOOSEBERRY: Hush, Goldie! Do you want us hanged as well as banished?

MRS. GOOSEBERRY: Banished? Who's been talking to you about banishment? Surely not the King. Why, you're the best gardener he's ever had.

MR. GOOSEBERRY *(Sighing deeply):* But this time he demands the impossible.

GOLDIE: Nothing is impossible for you, Father.

MR. GOOSEBERRY: His Majesty has commanded me to create a special tree in time for the Prince's birthday.

MRS. GOOSEBERRY: But that's the day after tomorrow!

MR. GOOSEBERRY: And he has further decreed that the

tree must be so beautiful and possess such charm that the Prince will want to spend all his waking hours in the garden.

MRS. GOOSEBERRY: But did you explain to the King how impossible that is?

MR. GOOSEBERRY: The King would hear no explanations. Either I produce such a tree or we shall be banished forever from Valentia.

MRS. GOOSEBERRY: How can he treat you so after a lifetime of faithful service?

GOLDIE: No kingdom in the world has such wonderful trees! And you have developed them all to please the Prince.

MRS. GOOSEBERRY: Remember the time you created the Lollipop Tree for the Prince?

GOLDIE: He spent days out here in the garden, stuffing himself with lollipops till he got a stomachache.

MRS. GOOSEBERRY: The same way with the Sugar Plum Tree and the Choc-a-Nut Tree.

GOLDIE: Then there was the Fig-a-Jig Tree and the Dreamland Tree, the Orange-Pineapple Tree and the wonderful Gumdrop Bush.

MRS. GOOSEBERRY: To say nothing of the Laughing Willow, the Golden Leaf Maple and the Penny-Bearing Pine.

MR. GOOSEBERRY (*Shaking his head sadly*): But none of those will help me now. Besides, the Prince lost interest in all of them, in a few days.

MRS. GOOSEBERRY: What must be, must be. You can only do your best. Now, come into the house for awhile and rest. Maybe you'll think of something.

MR. GOOSEBERRY: I *must* think of something. We can't leave our home and everything we have worked for all these years.

MRS. GOOSEBERRY *(Patting his shoulder):* There! There! Don't fret so.

GOLDIE: I'll stay outside and do a bit of weeding, Father. *(Cheerfully)* I'll try out your new garden hat. *(Takes hat and puts it on.* MR. *and* MRS. GOOSEBERRY *exit.* GOLDIE *pretends to look for weeds.)* Father is such a wonderful gardener, there are scarcely any weeds to be found. Oh, here are a few. *(Kneels and pretends to weed.* DALE *and* GAIL *enter.* DALE *carries a guidebook.)*

DALE: Excuse me. Is this the Royal Palace of Valentia?

GOLDIE *(Rising, in surprise):* Yes, it is. But who are you? No one is admitted here except on official business.

DALE: I am Dale Dawson, and this is my sister, Gail.

GAIL: We are American tourists. My brother and I are doing some sight-seeing of our own. Are you a member of the royal family?

GOLDIE: Goodness, no! I am Goldie Gooseberry. My father is the Royal Gardener.

GAIL: How exciting! You must see the King often.

GOLDIE: Yes, indeed. Sometimes too often. *(Claps her hand over her mouth)* Oh, dear! I shouldn't have said that.

DALE: Why not? Isn't Valentia a free country?

GAIL: Isn't the King a kind man?

GOLDIE: Oh, yes. The King is very kind . . . only . . . that is . . . well, *most* of the time he's very kind. He's been very good to Father and to us, too, until today.

DALE: I'm afraid we're asking too many questions. But, you see, we don't know very much about kings. We've never seen any.

GAIL: That's why we wanted to see a real palace and maybe get a glimpse of the King and Queen.

GOLDIE: Well, there isn't any Queen. She died several years ago. There's just the King and His Highness, the Prince.

DALE: How old is the Prince?

GOLDIE: His Highness will be ten years old day after tomorrow.

GAIL: That's Valentine's Day!

GOLDIE: Valentine's Day? What is that?

GAIL: Don't the people of Valentia celebrate the fourteenth of February?

GOLDIE: Oh, we celebrate it all right, but only because it's the birthday of His Royal Highness.

DALE: How strange! I thought every country in the world observed Valentine's Day.

GOLDIE: I've never even heard of it. What is it?

GAIL: Why, it's the day we send valentines to people we like.

GOLDIE: What are valentines?

DALE: They're little greeting cards, usually in the shape of hearts. Sometimes they're decorated with roses and cupids, and they always have verses that tell how much we love our friends and family. "Roses are red, violets are blue, sugar is sweet and so are you!"

GOLDIE *(Laughing):* I like that one.

GAIL: That's a very old one. We usually make up our own.

DALE: Maybe you should send your Prince a valentine, especially since it's his birthday.

GOLDIE: I wouldn't dare. And anyhow, we'll probably have to leave here on the Prince's birthday.

GAIL: But isn't this your home?

GOLDIE: Yes, but you see, the Prince is very sickly. He stays shut up in his room most of the time. His father, the King, wants him to spend more time in the garden, but the Prince hardly ever ventures out-of-doors. And that's where my father's trouble begins. He has created all sorts of rare and wonderful trees for the Prince's pleasure, but after a few days, he tires of them. Now the King has ordered him to develop a tree so marvelous that the Prince will spend hours and hours in the garden. Unless he can produce such a tree by February 14th, our whole family will be banished from Valentia forever.

DALE: That's terrible. Your king must be a most unreasonable man.

GAIL: Didn't your father tell him it takes a long time to develop a new tree?

GOLDIE: Of course. But the King has made up his mind!

GAIL: I wish we could help you. Surely there must be some way to make the King listen to reason.

DALE: What's the matter with the Prince? Why doesn't he want to stay in the garden? What does he do when he does come outside?

GOLDIE: Walks up and down the garden paths, or picks the flowers. Mostly he looks at the trees, especially the ones Father has developed.

DALE: That doesn't sound like much fun to me. Doesn't he play any games or invite any of his friends in to play with him?

GOLDIE (Shaking her head): He doesn't have any friends.

DALE: Why is he so unpopular?

GOLDIE: Oh, he isn't unpopular. Everybody loves him, especially the children. But, you see, he is the Prince. The King would never let him play with ordinary children.

DALE: I think your Prince is lonely, not sickly. No wonder he won't stay in the garden. There's nothing to do.

GAIL: Maybe he thinks no one likes him. How does he know the children love him if they never get a chance to tell him so?

DALE: What your prince seems to need is a Valentine party instead of a birthday party.

GAIL *(Excitedly):* Dale! Dale! I have a terrific idea. *(Whispers in his ear)*

DALE: They'd never go for it, not in a million years.

GAIL: But they have nothing to lose! If they're to be banished anyhow, what difference would it make?

GOLDIE: Can you help us?

GAIL: We have an idea that might work. Please let us talk to your father.

DALE: Remember, Gail, if we both land in the palace dungeon, it was *your* idea, not *ours.* But I'm willing to take a chance. Goldie, will you take us to your father?

GOLDIE: I know Father will be willing to try anything, if there's the slightest chance. *(Starts off)* It's only a few steps. *(Calling)* Father! Father! I'm bringing some friends to see you. Hurry, Mother! Open the door. *(All exit as curtains close.)*

*   *   *   *   *

SCENE 2

TIME: *February 14th.*

SETTING: *Same as Scene 1, except for a folding screen at center on which is hung a sign:* HAPPY BIRTHDAY, YOUR HIGHNESS!

AT RISE: MR. *and* MRS. GOOSEBERRY *are pacing back and forth in garden.*

MRS. GOOSEBERRY *(Wringing her hands):* This is the

craziest thing I have ever heard of. We shall all lose our heads before this day is done!

MR. GOOSEBERRY: Now, now, Mother! Calm yourself. As the children say, we have nothing to lose.

MRS. GOOSEBERRY *(Wryly):* Only our heads!

MR. GOOSEBERRY: Nonsense, my dear! No one has been beheaded in Valentia for a hundred years. *(GOLDIE enters.)*

GOLDIE: Is everything ready, Father?

MR. GOOSEBERRY: Everything in *my* department is ready. If only your friends from the strange land of America do their part.

GOLDIE: Oh, I know they will. When will the Prince and the King arrive?

MR. GOOSEBERRY: They should be here any minute now.

MRS. GOOSEBERRY: I know I'm going to faint!

MR. GOOSEBERRY: Then go in and lie down, my dear.

MRS. GOOSEBERRY: And miss all the excitement! I should say not! *(An offstage blast of trumpets is heard.)*

GOLDIE *(Jumping up and down):* They're coming! They're coming!

MRS. GOOSEBERRY *(Nervously):* Where are my smelling salts?

GOLDIE *(Calmly):* In your apron pocket. Keep your fingers crossed for good luck.

LORD CHANCELLOR *(Entering):* Make way! Make way for His Supreme Majesty, King Valentino, and His Royal Highness, the Prince of Valentia. *(KING and PRINCE enter, follow LORD CHANCELLOR to center.)*

KING *(To PRINCE):* In just a few seconds, you will see your birthday surprise.

PRINCE: I suppose it will be another tree!

KING (*Impatiently*): Of course it will be another tree, my son. But what a tree! This time, Mr. Gooseberry assures me, he has outdone himself. Although I have not seen it, I can safely say there is no other like it in the whole wide world. (*To* MR. GOOSEBERRY) Ah, Mr. Gooseberry, I see everything is ready. At the sound of the trumpets, let the ceremony begin! (*As trumpets sound offstage,* MR. *and* MRS. GOOSEBERRY *move to either side of folding screen.* GOLDIE *curtsies to* PRINCE.)

GOLDIE (*Reciting*):
> A happy birthday to our Prince,
> So noble, brave, and true!
> And now behold the Birthday Tree,
> Especially for you!

(MR. *and* MRS. GOOSEBERRY *remove screen, revealing a bare tree planted in a green tub.*)

PRINCE: What is it? There's not a leaf or flower on it!

LORD CHANCELLOR: Is this some sort of joke?

KING (*Angrily*): What is the meaning of this? Gooseberry, what do you have to say for yourself?

MRS. GOOSEBERRY: I begged him not to do such a thing, Your Majesty.

KING (*Shouting*): This is an outrage. Surely, you cannot mean that this is the Prince's Birthday Tree.

MR. GOOSEBERRY: If Your Majesty will grant me a few minutes, everything will be explained.

GOLDIE (*Calling offstage*): Gail! Dale! Let the March of the Children begin! (GAIL *and* DALE *enter, followed by a long procession of* CHILDREN, *each carrying a red heart attached to a wire hanger. They march around tree, singing to the tune of "Oats, Peas, Beans, and Barley Grow."*)

CHILDREN *(Singing)*:
>A happy birthday, Prince of mine,
>We want you for our Valentine.
>And now we offer you our hearts
>With all the love this day imparts.
>All happiness and joy be thine,
>If you will be our Valentine! *(Repeat)*

KING: What's this? What's this? A new national anthem?

MR. GOOSEBERRY *(Holding up his hand for quiet)*: Your Majesty *(Bows)* and Your Royal Highness *(Bows again)*, I present two visitors from a strange land— Dale Dawson and his sister, Gail, from the United States of America. They bring a message of the most vital importance.

DALE *(Bowing to each one in turn)*: Your Majesty, Your Royal Highness! Gail and I just happened to be touring through your wonderful country when we heard of the Royal Palace and the beautiful gardens, so we came to see them. When we arrived, Mr. Gooseberry and his daughter, Goldie, told us about the Prince's birthday falling on the fourteenth of February. In America and in many countries of the world, that day is celebrated as St. Valentine's Day.

PRINCE *(Surprised)*: You mean my birthday is celebrated in other lands and other countries?

DALE: Yes, Your Highness, and you are extremely fortunate to have been born on a day that is set aside for love and friendship, the two greatest gifts in the world.

PRINCE: But who was this St. Valentine you speak of?

GAIL: St. Valentine was a good and great man who was killed by his enemies on February 14th. It is said that a beautiful pink almond tree grew and blossomed over his grave. Ever since his death, people have sent messages of love and friendship to their dear ones on the day, which has become known as St. Valentine's Day.

PRINCE: Which is also my birthday?

DALE: Right! So when we heard that Mr. Gooseberry had been commanded to create a special tree in honor of your birthday, Gail suggested that he make you a Tree of Hearts, and here it is. *(During speeches by* GAIL *and* DALE, CHILDREN *have been hanging their hearts on tree branches.)*

GOLDIE *(With a curtsy to the* PRINCE*)*: Dear Prince, the children of Valentia love you with all their hearts. They welcome this opportunity to show you their love and loyalty. *(*CHILDREN *sing to tune of "The King of France with Forty Thousand Men.")*

CHILDREN *(Singing)*:
> The tree of hearts
> Is planted here to show
> Our noble Prince
> The children love you so!

PRINCE: I am deeply touched and honored. This tree is the most beautiful tree I have ever seen. I thank you with all my heart! *(Applauds)* Look, Father, see how each heart on the tree is decorated. *(Peering at it closely)* And there are verses on some of them. *(Reading)* "If you love me as I love you, no knife could cut our love in two!" How remarkable! Who is the author of this masterpiece?

GAIL: You don't have to sign your name to a valentine, Your Highness. It's sort of a secret.

KING *(Reading)*: And listen to this one, "I love you little, I love you big! With you I'd like to dance a jig!"

PRINCE *(Laughing)*: That's a good idea. I think I'd like to dance a jig with any of these young ladies.

LORD CHANCELLOR *(Reading verses on hearts)*: Here's a

noble sentiment. "When you are sad and feeling blue, remember, Prince, we all love you."

PRINCE: That's the best of all. It makes me feel happy all over. I never knew I had so many friends before.

DALE: That's the whole idea of Valentine's Day, Your Highness. When you love somebody, that's the day you can tell him so without feeling shy or silly.

PRINCE: It will take me days to read all these verses.

GAIL: And days more to answer them. You see, Your Highness, Valentine's Day is a two-way proposition. The joy is not only in receiving them, the best part is in sending them.

PRINCE: A wonderful idea! Chancellor, get me paper and pencil at once. I must compose some verses.

MR. GOOSEBERRY: I have another suggestion.

KING: Whatever it is, Gooseberry, feel free to make it. Your Tree of Hearts is the most magnificent thing you have ever done! Chancellor, make a note to build the Gooseberrys the finest cottage in the land.

MRS. GOOSEBERRY (Happily): Then you are not sending us away, Your Majesty?

KING: Sending you away, indeed! The Prince will want a Tree of Hearts every year after this, and perhaps the Chancellor and I would each like one of our own.

MR. GOOSEBERRY: As our little friends from America have pointed out, friendship is, indeed, a sheltering tree. And now for my suggestion.

KING: Chancellor, take pen in hand.

MR. GOOSEBERRY: I suggest first of all, that we turn the rest of the day over to Dale and Gail to be celebrated in the fashion of a true Valentine party. (Applause) Mrs. Gooseberry has baked some heart-shaped cakes for the occasion and Goldie is ready to serve ice cream in heart shapes. (Applause)

KING: Very good ! Excellent!

MR. GOOSEBERRY: And one further suggestion, Sire, about the care of the tree. A Tree of Hearts is not like other trees. It needs more than water and sunshine. It must have plenty of love and attention. It must always be within range of the sound of laughter, and what it needs most is children playing underneath its branches. Without this kind of care, it will wither and die.

KING: Chancellor, prepare an edict. The Palace Garden henceforth is open every day to all children who wish to come inside and play with the Prince. *(Applause)*

PRINCE: Thank you, Father, thank you. This is the happiest birthday I have ever had. In fact, thanks to Gail and Dale, and the Gooseberrys and the Tree of Hearts, this is the happiest day of my life. Nevertheless, I have one more request.

KING: Whatever it is, it shall be granted, my son.

PRINCE: It is very simple. I merely wish to change my name from Prince Valentino to Prince Valentine in memory of the good saint we honor on my birthday.

KING: It shall be done. Chancellor, make the official pronouncement.

LORD CHANCELLOR: Hear ye! Hear ye! From this day forth, the Crown Prince and Heir Apparent to the crown of Valentia shall be known as Prince Valentine.

DALE: Three cheers for Prince Valentine! *(Curtains close as CHILDREN dance around the Tree of Hearts, cheering.)*

THE END

The Birthday Pie

Characters

GEORGE WASHINGTON SMITH
MRS. SMITH, *his mother*
BETTY SMITH, *his sister*
TRUDY
ANNE
BILLY
HARRY
FRED } *his friends*
NANCY
BOB
BETSY
STEVE

TIME: *February 22nd.*

SETTING: *The Smith living room. Couch, chairs, tables make up the furnishings. Large table and ten chairs are center. Table is set with red, white, and blue napkins and small placecards. Centerpiece is a hatchet with American flags.*

AT RISE: GEORGE *is slumped in chair, unhappily twiddling with small radio.* BETTY *is arranging napkins at place settings.*

BETTY: You'd better hurry up and dress, George.

GEORGE: I don't feel like dressing.

BETTY: But it's almost time for your birthday party. The guests will soon be here.

GEORGE: I don't feel like having a birthday party.

BETTY: What's the matter with you? Are you sick?

GEORGE: I think I have the birthday blues.

BETTY: You'd better not let Mother hear you say that. She's worked very hard on your party.

GEORGE: Who said I ever wanted a party?

BETTY: But it wouldn't be a birthday without a party.

GEORGE: I don't even want a birthday.

BETTY: George Washington Smith! I never heard such silly talk.

GEORGE: And I never heard such a silly name! George Washington Smith!

BETTY: George Washington is a very famous name. It's a great name for any American.

GEORGE: But it just doesn't go with Smith. Why did I have to be born on the twenty-second of February?

BETTY: Well, you were, so stop fussing and go get dressed.

MRS. SMITH: The table looks lovely, Betty. *(Turns and sees* GEORGE*)* George! You aren't dressed for the party. Now, go and put on your good suit.

GEORGE: All right, Mother. *(From door)* Are we having cherry pie again this year?

MRS. SMITH: Of course, dear.

GEORGE *(Groaning):* I might have known! *(Exits)*

MRS. SMITH: Now what did he mean by that?

BETTY: Pay no attention to George, Mother. He's just annoyed about everything—mostly his name.

MRS. SMITH: I think George is a fine name for a boy.

BETTY: He doesn't mind the *George* by itself. It's the

Washington he doesn't like—*George Washington Smith!*

MRS. SMITH: But my name was *Washington* before I was married. I never minded being called *Martha Washington* when I was a child. *(Suddenly)* I hope those pies cool in time for the party. I have them on the back porch.

BETTY: Your pies are always wonderful, Mother. Hot or cold. *(Doorbell rings.)*

MRS. SMITH *(Calling):* George, hurry up. Your guests are arriving.

BETTY: I'll answer the door, Mother. *(Exits and re-enters with* TRUDY, ANNE, *and* BILLY, *each carrying a present.)*

TRUDY: Hello, Mrs. Smith.

ANNE: Oh, the table looks so pretty!

MRS. SMITH: I'm glad to see you all.

BILLY: Where shall we put our presents, Mrs. Smith? Can we put them in another room for now, and bring them in later as a surprise?

MRS. SMITH: That's a wonderful idea, Billy. Trudy, would you and Anne please take the others around to the sun porch. You can put the gifts and coats in there. *(Exits)*

BETTY *(Ushering in* HARRY *and* FRED*):* Make yourselves at home. George will be down soon.

TRUDY: Hello, everyone! Anne and I will take your coats. *(*ANNE *and* TRUDY *exit and re-enter immediately.)*

HARRY: Hi, Billy.

BILLY: Hi, Harry, Fred. *(To* BETTY*)* Where's George?

BETTY: I don't know what's keeping him. I'll run upstairs and see. *(Exits right. Doorbell rings.)*

BILLY: I'll get it. *(Exits right and re-enters, followed by* NANCY, BOB, BETSY *and* STEVE. TRUDY *and* ANNE *exchange greetings with them, take their coats, exit, and re-enter.)*

NANCY: Oh, isn't the table pretty?

BOB: I hope we eat soon. I'm starved!

BETSY: Bob Freeman! What would Mother say?

STEVE: My mother gave me such a lecture on manners I'm afraid to move. *(MRS. SMITH enters.)*

ALL: Hello, Mrs. Smith!

MRS. SMITH: I'm glad to see all of you. *(Looking around)* Isn't George down yet? What can be keeping him? *(BETTY enters right.)*

BETTY: Where in the world is George? He isn't in his room. *(GEORGE enters from left.)*

GEORGE: Hello, everybody. Sorry I'm late.

ALL: Happy Birthday, George.

BETTY: Find your places at the table. I made placecards for everybody. *(Children start to walk around table, looking for their placecards.)*

MRS. SMITH: I'll need you to help with the refreshments, Betty. *(All sit as they find places. BETTY and MRS. SMITH exit.)*

NANCY *(Looking at her placecard):* Each placecard has a rhyme, but the last word is missing. See if you can guess what mine is. *(Reads)*

> Mistress Nancy, take this chair,
> And have a lot of fun.
> This is a double party
> For George and—

ALL: Washington!

TRUDY: This is like a game. Let me read mine. *(Reads)*

> Welcome, little Trudy,
> Upon this happy day,
> And give three cheers for Washington,
> Hip-hip, hip-hip—

ALL: Hooray!

BOB: Now it's my turn. *(Reads)*

    This place is for our Robert.

    We hope he is content.

    Who knows but someday, years from now,

    He may be—

ALL: President!

BILLY: I can tell you right now I'm not going to vote for him. *(Laughs)* Now let me read mine. *(Reads)*

    This place reserved for Billy,

    A very special guest.

    I know he thinks these colors,

    Red, white and blue, are—

ALL: Best!

BETSY: My turn! *(Reads)*

    Here sits a girl named Betsy.

    Her spirits never lag.

    A lady with a name like hers

    First made our country's—

ALL: Flag!

HARRY: I have a funny one. *(Reads)*

    Harry, you're the next in line,

    So sit where you are beckoned.

    Harry has a birthday too,

    But not on the—

ALL: Twenty-second!

ANNE: These rhymes took a lot of work. Here's mine. *(Reads)*

    Anne is such a pretty name,

    We're glad to have her here.

    She knows the name of Washington

    Is one to make us—

ALL: Cheer!

FRED: My rhyme is about the table decorations. *(Reads)*

Howdy, Fred, please take a seat,
And look around and see
The hatchet with which little George
Cut down the cherry—

ALL: Tree!

STEVE: I guess I'm the last one. *(Reads)*
Our friendly Steve will sit right here
And help to celebrate
The birthday of a famous pair
Born on this lucky—

ALL: Date!

BILLY: Don't you have a rhyme, George?

GEORGE: Yes, mine has two verses. *(Reads)*
And here's our host whose name is George.
He waits for cherry pie,
And like that other famous George,
He cannot tell a lie.

His name will always make him think
Of that inspiring youth—
The other famous Washington
Who always told the—

ALL: Truth! *(BETTY enters, carrying large birthday cake, decorated with a ring of red cherries on white frosting. She sets cake on table in front of GEORGE.)*

GEORGE *(Excitedly):* A cake! A birthday cake! *(MRS. SMITH enters with plates of ice cream on tray, which she sets down on small table.)*

MRS. SMITH *(As she begins to serve ice cream):* I hope the cake is all right.

TRUDY: I'm sure it's wonderful, Mrs. Smith. You're such a good cook.

ANNE: Let's all sing "Happy Birthday!" *(All join in singing of song.)*

BILLY *(Eyeing cake hungrily):* This cake looks great, but nobody can bake cherry pies like yours, Mrs. Smith.

BOB: Cherry pies! Yum! That's one reason I always like George's birthday parties. We always have cherry pie!

BETSY: Bob Freeman! What a thing to say!

MRS. SMITH: That's all right, Bob. We were going to have cherry pie today, but a terrible thing happened.

BILLY: What?

STEVE: Did you burn them?

MRS. SMITH: No, but I was late in baking them, and I set them out on the back porch to cool. When I went for them, they were gone—just disappeared.

ALL *(Ad lib):* How awful! That's terrible! Too bad. *(Etc.)*

MRS. SMITH: I simply can't understand it. The porch is screened in.

ANNE: That's too bad, Mrs. Smith, but don't worry. We all love cake.

BOB: But think of all those cherry pies!

NANCY: How did you ever manage to bake a cake in such a short time?

MRS. SMITH: I didn't. Betty had to run up to the bakery and buy one.

BETTY: Aren't you going to cut the cake, George?

GEORGE *(Pushing the cake away from him):* I—I can't. I don't think I feel very well.

MRS. SMITH: What's the matter, George? Are you sick?

GEORGE: Yes—er—that is—no—no, I'm not sick. *(Throwing down his napkin in disgust)* How can a guy lie a little when his name is *George Washington Smith!*

BETTY: Lie?

MRS. SMITH: What are you talking about?

GEORGE: I'm talking about the pies. Oh, Mom, I'm so ashamed of myself. But—well—I've always hated having cherry pie and ice cream for my birthday, when all the other kids have a birthday cake, so I—I sneaked out on the porch when I was supposed to be getting dressed, and—

MRS. SMITH *(Angrily):* George Washington Smith! What did you do with those pies?

GEORGE: I hid them. I took them down to the cellar and hid them on the top shelf behind the strawberry jam.

BETTY: George! What a terrible thing to do!

GEORGE *(Ashamed):* I know, and I'm sorry, Mom, honest. I never dreamed you would go out and buy a cake.

MRS. SMITH: And I never dreamed you wanted a birthday cake so badly that you would do a thing like that. Maybe I was thinking too much about George Washington and the cherry tree.

STEVE: Our teacher says that story didn't really happen anyhow.

GEORGE: I don't care if it really happened or if somebody made it up. I'm glad I know about it, because it helped me to tell the truth and get that funny feeling out of my stomach.

MRS. SMITH *(Smiling):* So am I, dear. It's a wonderful story to grow on.

BOB: I always wished I had been named for somebody famous, but maybe it's pretty hard to live up to a great name.

GEORGE: From now on, I'm going to try to live up to mine. Maybe some day George Washington Smith will be a great name, too.

MRS. SMITH: I'm sure it will. But, Betty, what are we waiting for? Now that we know where the pies are, we can serve them.

TRUDY: But this lovely cake!

BOB: I vote for the cherry pie!

ALL *(Ad lib):* So do we! Me, too! We want cherry pie! *(Etc.)*

MRS. SMITH: Don't worry about the cake, children. We'll save that for supper, and we'll have our birthday pie now after all.

STEVE *(Rising):* Let's have a song in honor of Mrs. Smith. Do you all know "Billy Boy"?

ALL *(Ad lib):* Sure. That's a good song! *(Etc.)*

STEVE: Then here we go! *(Children rise and sing to tune of "Billy Boy.")*

ALL *(Singing):*
She can bake a cherry pie, Georgie Boy, Georgie Boy.
She can bake a cherry pie, Mister Georgie.
She can bake a cherry pie quick as you can wink your eye
There is no one who can ever beat your mother!
(They continue singing, as curtain falls.)

THE END

The Mount Vernon Cricket

Characters

LAUREL BAILEY
SHIRLEY ⎤
DRINA ⎟
DEAN ⎬ *her friends*
ARTHUR ⎟
JACK ⎦
MR. BAILEY ⎤ *her parents*
MRS. BAILEY ⎦
MR. HARVEY, *a real estate agent*
MRS. SIMPSON, *a neighbor*

TIME: *February.*
SETTING: *Living room of the Bailey home. Sofa is center, with coffee table in front of it. Armchairs, tables, and telephone complete the furnishings. Exit left leads to front door; exit right to rest of house.*
AT RISE: LAUREL, SHIRLEY, DRINA, ARTHUR, *and* DEAN, *wearing coats and jackets, enter left.*
SHIRLEY: Well, here we are. Now let's see it.
DRINA: I still don't believe it.
ARTHUR: Neither do I.
DEAN: Who ever heard of a cricket in *February*?

LAUREL: It's not a real cricket. It's a footstool.

DEAN: Does it have six legs?

LAUREL: Of course not!

DEAN: Then it's not a cricket. A cricket is an insect and insects have six legs.

LAUREL: But this is *not* an insect! It's a piece of furniture.

ARTHUR: Then why is it called a *cricket*?

LAUREL: Cricket is just an old-fashioned word for an old-fashioned stool. I'll run up to my room and get it. *(LAUREL exits right. Others take off coats and fling them on sofa.)*

SHIRLEY: Do you really believe Laurel has a footstool from Mount Vernon that belonged to George Washington?

ARTHUR: Of course not. You know Laurel and her imagination.

DEAN: Sh! Here she comes. *(LAUREL re-enters, carrying an old-fashioned footstool.)*

LAUREL: Well, here it is. I'm keeping it in my room for now, but when we move into our new house, it will go by the fireplace. *(She puts stool on floor.)*

DRINA: What new house?

LAUREL: It isn't really a new house. It's the old Martin place my parents are going to buy.

ARTHUR: That wreck!

LAUREL: Mr. Harvey, the real estate agent, says there's not a crack in the walls and the foundation is solid as a rock.

SHIRLEY: Why are we talking about old houses? It's an old cricket we came to see.

LAUREL: Mother says this is solid cherry.

DEAN *(Sarcastically):* No doubt made from the famous Washington cherry tree!

LAUREL: Don't be funny. *(Turns stool upside down)* Look. Here are Washington's initials.

DEAN *(Examining it):* That's what it says—"G.W."

ARTHUR *(Looking):* And there are some numbers—not very clear, but I can make out a one and a seven. That would be seventeen hundred and something!

SHIRLEY: George Washington was born in 1732.

DRINA: Maybe it did belong to George Washington, after all. *(JACK rushes in.)*

JACK *(Huffing and puffing):* Boy, am I glad your front door was open!

DRINA: What's the matter?

JACK: I just cut through old Mrs. Simpson's backyard, and that rickety gate of hers came right off its hinges!

DEAN: Do you think she saw you, Jack?

JACK: She couldn't miss me. She was standing at her kitchen window. But I was going so fast that she'll never recognize me.

ARTHUR: Let's hope not. You know how Mrs. Simpson hates to have anyone cut through her yard.

JACK: I hope she doesn't catch up with me and tell Dad. Do you mind if I stay here awhile, Laurel?

LAUREL: Of course not. *(JACK takes jacket off, puts it on sofa.)*

DEAN: Take a look at Laurel's latest antique.

JACK: What is it?

DEAN: A footstool that belonged to George Washington.

DRINA: It even has George Washington's initials on it.

JACK: Let me see it. *(Examines stool)* This ought to be in a museum.

SHIRLEY: We don't have any antiques in our house. My dad says they break if you look at them.

JACK: I'll bet this one wouldn't. It's solid as a rock. *(Sits on it)* See? It doesn't even wiggle. *(Doorbell rings.)*

LAUREL: Excuse me. *(Exits left)*

JACK: I never thought I'd be sitting on a George Washington footstool or a George Washington anything.

MRS. SIMPSON *(Offstage):* I know he's in here. I saw him run up on your porch!

DRINA: It's Mrs. Simpson. You'd better go out the back door, Jack.

DEAN: No! Just sit tight. She'll never be able to pick you out. *(*MRS. SIMPSON *rushes in, followed by* LAUREL.*)*

LAUREL: Really, Mrs. Simpson. Mother's not here.

MRS. SIMPSON: I'm not here to see your mother. I'm here to collar the boy who broke my gate and snapped the limb off my lilac bush. *(Seeing boys)* Aha! There you are. Which one of you did it?

SHIRLEY: Are you sure it was one of them, Mrs. Simpson?

MRS. SIMPSON: Yes, it had to be. Vandalism. Sheer vandalism.

LAUREL: Oh, no, Mrs. Simpson. It must have been an accident. I'm sure no one would have damaged your property on purpose.

MRS. SIMPSON: That's a matter for the police to decide.

ALL: The police!

MRS. SIMPSON: As soon as I discover the guilty party, I'm going straight to the police. Trespassing is no accident. Now! Who did it?

JACK: I did, Mrs. Simpson, and I'm sorry. I really didn't mean to break your gate. *(Stands)*

MRS. SIMPSON: I might have known it was you, Jack Roberts.

JACK: I'll be glad to fix it for you, or I can pay to have it fixed out of my allowance.

MRS. SIMPSON *(Angrily):* You won't get out of it that easily, young man. I'm going straight home and report this. *(As she turns to go, she stumbles.)*

LAUREL *(Grabbing her arm):* Look out, Mrs. Simpson. Your shoelace is untied. Sit down here and I'll tie it for you. *(Seats* MRS. SIMPSON *on stool)*

MRS. SIMPSON: Is this a new stool? I don't remember seeing it before.

LAUREL: It's Mother's latest antique find, Mrs. Simpson. It came from Mount Vernon. *(*LAUREL *kneels to tie shoelace.)*

DRINA: And it has George Washington's initials carved on the bottom.

MRS. SIMPSON: Really?

LAUREL: There! Your shoelace is tied good and tight now. *(Stands)*

MRS. SIMPSON: Thank you. I think I'll just sit here a minute and catch my breath. All that excitement over my gate and lilac bush . . . .

JACK: I admit breaking your gate, Mrs. Simpson, but I never touched that lilac bush!

MRS. SIMPSON: Of course you didn't. That limb snapped off with the heavy snow we had last week.

ARTHUR: But you just blamed Jack for it!

MRS. SIMPSON *(Rubbing her forehead):* Then I was mistaken. It was the snow. And as for that gate, the hinge has been loose for a month. It almost fell off when the mailman came yesterday.

JACK: Then I really wasn't to blame?

MRS. SIMPSON: Well, you shouldn't have cut through my yard, but as for the gate, it would have come off sooner or later. *(Rising)* Oops! I feel a bit dizzy.

ARTHUR: Here, take my arm.

MRS. SIMPSON: Thank you, young man.

JACK: I'll still be glad to fix your gate, Mrs. Simpson.

DEAN: My dad has a pair of hinges he's not using.

MRS. SIMPSON: I just might accept your offer. Oh, well, I guess boys will be boys!

SHIRLEY: Even George Washington chopped down that cherry tree, you know.

MRS. SIMPSON: Pure legend, my dear, but a legend we like to believe. It shows the value of telling the truth. Since Jack has been so truthful, I guess I can afford to overlook the trespassing.

JACK: Thanks, Mrs. Simpson.

MRS. SIMPSON: Goodbye, everyone. *(Exits)*

DEAN: Jack, why did you suddenly own up to breaking her gate when you ducked in here to avoid getting caught?

JACK: I don't know exactly. It's a funny thing, but the truth popped out almost before I knew it.

DRINA: And Mrs. Simpson—I thought wild horses couldn't get her to admit she was wrong.

SHIRLEY *(Staring at stool):* Do you suppose . . . No, no, it couldn't be possible!

LAUREL: What couldn't be possible, Shirley?

SHIRLEY: I was just thinking that both Jack and Mrs. Simpson were sitting on the George Washington cricket when they blurted out the truth.

DRINA: It happened twice.

ARTHUR *(Sitting on stool):* Well, I'll bet it won't happen the third time. Not while I'm sitting here. Go ahead and try me.

LAUREL: You're naturally a truthful person, Arthur.

SHIRLEY: Arthur does exaggerate every now and then.

ARTHUR: What do you mean—exaggerate?

DEAN: Remember that picture of Babe Ruth you're always showing people?

ARTHUR *(Drawing picture from pocket):* You mean this one?

DEAN: The one with the autograph—"Best regards from Babe Ruth."

ARTHUR: I got it from my grandfather.

JACK: Who knew the Babe, right?

ARTHUR *(Uneasily):* Well, no, not exactly . . . . My grandfather went to see the Yankees play and after the game they were selling autographed pictures, so he bought one for me.

DEAN: So that's how it happened.

ARTHUR: Sure.

JACK *(With a mock bow):* Footstool, I salute you. You finally got the truth out of him.

ARTHUR *(Jumping up):* Do you mean I haven't been telling the truth about that picture?

DEAN: About the picture, yes—but not about your grandfather. You had us all believing that he and the Babe were pals.

ARTHUR: But I never said that.

JACK: That's the impression you gave.

ARTHUR: I guess everybody stretches the truth once in a while . . . .

LAUREL: Not when he's sitting on the Mount Vernon cricket!

DEAN: I'm beginning to think there *is* something special about that stool.

LAUREL: Wait till Mother hears about this. *(MR. and MRS. BAILEY enter left, each carrying a large, ugly vase.)*

MRS. BAILEY: Wait till Mother hears about what, Laurel? Hello, everyone. I see you brought down the old footstool.

LAUREL: And wait till you hear what's happened, Mother.

MRS. BAILEY: Wait till you see what I've just bought. Do be careful, Jim. Set it here on the table. *(She puts her vase on table.* MR. BAILEY *puts his beside it and removes his coat.)*

MR. BAILEY: Your mother can't pass an antique shop without buying something. *(Phone rings.)*

MRS. BAILEY: I'll get it. *(Takes off her coat and hands it to* MR. BAILEY, *as she picks up receiver)* Hello . . . . Oh, yes, Mr. Harvey . . . . Well, yes, as far as I know. *(Puts hand over mouthpiece)* It's Mr. Harvey, Jim. He has the final papers for the Martin house. Wants to know if he can stop by in a few minutes.

MR. BAILEY: Fine. Tell him to come ahead. I'll get everything we need out of my desk. *(*MR. BAILEY *exits right.)*

MRS. BAILEY *(On phone):* That will be fine, Mr. Harvey. We'll expect you. Goodbye. *(Hangs up)* He wants to close the deal this afternoon. *(Starts toward exit)* I think I'll make some coffee. It's such a cold day. *(Exits)*

DRINA: Your parents are going to be busy. I think we'd better go. Come on, Shirley. *(Girls put on coats.)*

JACK: What do you say we fix Mrs. Simpson's gate right away. Let's go. *(Boys put on coats.)*

ARTHUR: O.K. So long, Laurel. Don't let your folks be talked into a quick deal on that house. Mr. Harvey probably stretches the truth as much as I do.

LAUREL: They're not likely to ask my advice, Arthur. But I just might give Mr. Harvey the cricket test. 'Bye, everybody. See you later. *(They exit left, as* MRS. BAILEY *enters right.)*

MRS. BAILEY: We'd better straighten up a bit before Mr. Harvey arrives.

LAUREL: Mother, there's something I'd like to ask you.

MRS. BAILEY: Not now, dear. And please take this stool upstairs.

LAUREL: But it's the stool I want to ask you about.

MRS. BAILEY: I said not now, dear. Please get this stool out of the way. It doesn't belong here.

LAUREL: Can't it just stay down here till after Mr. Harvey leaves?

MRS. BAILEY *(Impatiently):* I don't know what has come over you, Laurel. I want the room to look nice when Mr. Harvey comes. *(Doorbell rings)* Oh, dear! There he is now. You answer the door, Laurel, while I get the coffee. *(She exits right.)*

LAUREL: Saved by the bell! *(She exits left and returns with* MR. HARVEY, *who wears an overcoat and carries a briefcase.)* Come in, Mr. Harvey. Let me take your coat.

MR. HARVEY: Thank you, Laurel. *(Removes coat)* Brr! It's cold outside. Nice and warm in here.

LAUREL: Won't you sit down? My parents will be here in a minute. *(*MR. HARVEY *sits in chair, briefcase in his lap.)*

MR. HARVEY: Thank you.

LAUREL: Let me take your briefcase, Mr. Harvey. *(She takes it and places it on footstool, which she moves beside his chair.)* I'll put it right here on the Mount Vernon cricket.

MR. HARVEY: The what?

LAUREL *(Laughing):* On our footstool from Mount Vernon, Mr. Harvey. It has George Washington's initials on the bottom. *(Shows initials to* MR. HARVEY, *then replaces stool with briefcase on it)*

MR. HARVEY: Well, what do you know! George Washington, who never told a lie. *(*MR. *and* MRS. BAILEY *enter.* MR. BAILEY *has papers in his hand. She carries coffee tray, which she sets on table.)*

MR. BAILEY: Hello, Mr. Harvey. Good to see you. *(Holding up papers he is carrying)* I think I have all the papers we'll need.

MRS. BAILEY: Good afternoon, Mr. Harvey. I'm so excited about the old Martin house, I can hardly wait to sign the agreement.

MR. HARVEY: I'm ready, too.

MRS. BAILEY: Let me give you a cup of coffee.

MR. HARVEY: Thank you. I'll drink to the new owners of the Martin place. *(She pours coffee and puts cup on table beside him. He turns to open briefcase.)* The blacker the day, the blacker the deed, I always say.

MR. BAILEY *(Sharply):* I hope there's nothing black about this deed, Harvey.

MR. HARVEY: Oh—er—certainly not. *(Fumbles with papers in case)* Now let me see, where is that original deed? I know it was right here. (LAUREL *picks up stool with briefcase and sets it on* MR. HARVEY's *lap.)*

LAUREL: Let me help you, Mr. Harvey.

MRS. BAILEY: Laurel, Mr. Harvey doesn't want that stool on his lap.

MR. HARVEY: Oh, yes, yes. I'm quite honored, as a matter of fact. *(Rummages through papers)* Here's the deed. Of course, you realize that the one wing of the house was built after the great fire.

MRS. BAILEY: Fire! I never knew there was a fire at the Martin place.

MR. HARVEY: Quite a bad one, back in the 1880's. Lightning did a lot of damage, too, but the walls have been reinforced.

MR. BAILEY: What's this about lightning and reinforced walls?

MR. HARVEY: Surely we mentioned that when we were talking about the foundation.

MRS. BAILEY: Good grief! What's wrong with the foundation?

MR. HARVEY: Well, as the house settled after the flood of '92 . . .

MRS. BAILEY: Fire and flood!

MR. BAILEY: Next thing you'll tell us there was an earthquake!

MR. HARVEY: Oh, no! Never an earthquake, although the chimneys were weakened by the hurricane a few years ago.

MR. BAILEY: Harvey, what are you trying to tell us?

MR. HARVEY: Actually, I don't know. But you and your wife are such nice people, and, well, to be quite honest about it, that Martin house is a real wreck.

MR. *and* MRS. BAILEY: What? But you said . . .

MR. HARVEY: I know, I know. I said a lot of things. But take my word for it—that place isn't worth half the price we're asking for it. Now the Collins house is something else again.

MR. BAILEY: You know we could never afford that, Harvey.

MRS. BAILEY: The garden is beautiful, and I understand the house has just been done over. I'd adore it, but it's very expensive, I'm sure.

MR. HARVEY: You're right. But I'd let you have the Collins house at the Martin place figure.

MR. BAILEY: Do you really mean it?

MR. HARVEY: I feel I should, after not telling you the facts about the Martin house.

MRS. BAILEY: Oh, Jim! Could we at least go look at it?

MR. BAILEY: Why not? *(To* MR. HARVEY*)* When can we see it, Harvey?

MR. HARVEY: First thing in the morning. *(Putting papers into briefcase)* And now, if you will excuse me, I must be going. I don't quite feel like myself.

LAUREL: Let me take that stool away, Mr. Harvey. *(She does so.)*

MR. HARVEY *(Looking at it):* A most remarkable piece of furniture, if you don't mind my saying so, Mrs. Bailey.

MRS. BAILEY: I didn't know you liked antiques, Mr. Harvey.

MR. HARVEY: I never did, especially. *(Puts his coat on)* Thanks for the coffee, Mrs. Bailey. I'll pick you up at 9:30 tomorrow morning.

MR. BAILEY: Fine. Goodbye.

LAUREL: I'll see you out, Mr. Harvey. *(She exits left with MR. HARVEY.)*

MRS. BAILEY: Well! That was the most amazing experience I've ever had in my life.

MR. BAILEY *(Puzzled):* I don't get it. First Harvey built up that Martin place and then gave us the facts about the walls and foundation just when we were going to sign the purchase agreement. I don't understand it.

LAUREL *(Re-entering):* I do, Dad. It was the stool.

MR. BAILEY: What are you talking about?

LAUREL *(Picking up stool):* I knew Mr. Harvey would have to tell the truth when I showed him George Washington's initials.

MRS. BAILEY: George Washington's initials? What do you mean?

LAUREL: You should know, Mother. You're the one who brought it from Mount Vernon.

MRS. BAILEY: Of course, I did . . . Mount Vernon, New York. The G.W. on the bottom stands for George Williams, a distant cousin of ours. He made it when he was seventeen years old!

LAUREL: You mean this stool has nothing to do with George Washington?

MRS. BAILEY: Absolutely nothing! Whatever gave you such an idea?

LAUREL: But it works, Mother. You saw yourself how it made Mr. Harvey tell the truth.

MR. BAILEY: Ridiculous!

LAUREL: It's not ridiculous, Dad. The minute I told Mr. Harvey the footstool was George Washington's and showed him the initials, he began to change.

MR. BAILEY: You actually told Harvey the cricket belonged to George Washington?

LAUREL: That's what I told everybody.

MRS. BAILEY: But, Laurel, how could you?

LAUREL: But I believed it, Mother, and so did they— Jack and Arthur and Mrs. Simpson—they all came out with the truth when they touched the stool.

MRS. BAILEY: This cricket was never even close to Washington's Mount Vernon.

LAUREL: Then why did it make everyone suddenly tell the truth?

MR. BAILEY: Perhaps George Washington set an example for telling the truth that they found hard to resist. In Harvey's case, I simply think his better nature took over.

MRS. BAILEY *(Thoughtfully):* You planted the George Washington idea in their minds, and they acted accordingly—the power of suggestion.

LAUREL: I suppose I'll have to call my friends and tell them I made a mistake. But I still think that stool has some mysterious power.

MRS. BAILEY *(Holding stool and smiling):* I thought you stopped believing in magic long ago.

MR. BAILEY: Let's give it another test. *(To* MRS.

BAILEY) Betty, just how much did you really pay for those vases?

MRS. BAILEY *(Floundering):* Why—er—didn't I tell you, dear? They were seventeen—er—I mean seventy-five dollars.

MR. BAILEY *(Frowning):* Hm-m. I thought I heard you mention a much lower figure. *(Smiling)* But I really don't care. With this wonderful bargain on the Collins house, you can buy an antique for every room in our new house. Just as long as you give the Mount Vernon cricket a place of honor.

LAUREL: That will be perfect, Mother—a cricket by the hearth. *(Curtain)*

THE END

The White House Rabbit

Characters

MR. RABBIT ⎫
PETER RABBIT ⎪
FLOPSY ⎪
MOPSY ⎬ *rabbits*
THUMPER ⎪
WHISKERS ⎪
COTTONTAIL ⎭
SCOTT HAYES ⎫ *President's children*
FANNY HAYES ⎭
CHARLES, *the White House gardener*
PIERRE ⎫ *visitors*
MARIE ⎭

MRS. RUTHERFORD B. HAYES, *the First Lady*

TIME: *1880.*
SETTING: *A corner of the White House lawn. Shrubbery is at right. At left is garden bench, and mounted on a post pointing off left is a sign reading* TO THE WHITE HOUSE.
AT RISE: *Parade of rabbits—*PETER RABBIT, FLOPSY, MOPSY, THUMPER, WHISKERS, *and* COTTONTAIL—*is*

filing past MR. RABBIT, *who stands center, writing in a notebook. Each rabbit carries basket of eggs.*

MR. RABBIT *(To audience):* I suppose all of you have heard about the tradition of Easter egg rolling on the White House lawn, and you may have wondered how it all started.

Well, the history books say that Rutherford B. Hayes was the first President to welcome children to the White House lawn back in 1878—but what they don't say is *who* gave President Hayes the idea for the egg rolling. . . .

Today, we're going to tell you who really started it all. . . . *(To* RABBITS*)*
> Hurry, hurry,
> Scurry, scurry,
> Rabbits on the run!
> Hustle, bustle,
> Bustle, hustle,
> Get your day's work done!

PETER RABBIT *(Mopping his brow):*
> With basket and barrow,
> With wagon and cart,
> Each Easter Bunny
> Is doing his part!

THUMPER:
> With yellow and purple,
> And red, white, and blue,
> We've dyed all the Easter eggs,
> Just to please you!

MR. RABBIT: But we must have more! *(Louder)* More! More! *More!*

FLOPSY: We have more eggs now than we know what to do with!

MR. RABBIT: I know what to do with them. I have a plan!

COTTONTAIL: What is it? Tell us!

MR. RABBIT: Not yet. It's a secret.

COTTONTAIL: We won't haul any more eggs until you tell us.

MR. RABBIT: That's no way for Easter rabbits to act. *(Pointing)* Take this load of eggs behind those bushes and hide them in the grass. When you bring in your next load, I may have some news for you. All right?

FLOPSY: It's a bargain! *(Rabbits continue off stage.* MR. RABBIT *stops* MOPSY. THUMPER *and* FLOPSY *pause.)*

MR. RABBIT: Mopsy, how many eggs do you have in your basket?

MOPSY: Two dozen. And not a one of them cracked.

MR. RABBIT: Good!

THUMPER: Look at mine, Mr. Rabbit. I made them red, white, and blue like the flag, because they're White House Easter eggs.

MR. RABBIT: That's a fine idea, Thumper. *(*THUMPER *exits.)*

FLOPSY: And I made mine pink, the First Lady's favorite color.

MR. RABBIT: I'm sure Mrs. Hayes will be pleased. Now hurry and hide these.

FLOPSY: Very well, Mr. Rabbit. But I still don't understand why you want so many eggs this year. Little Scott and Fanny Hayes won't know what to do with all of them.

MR. RABBIT: Leave them to me, Flopsy. You just go hide them.

FLOPSY: You're the boss, Mr. Rabbit. *(Exits)*

MR. RABBIT *(Figuring in notebook)*: Thirty-two, forty-two, seventy-two, one hundred! Not enough!

SCOTT *and* FANNY *(Rushing in)*: Mr. Rabbit! Mr. Rabbit!

MR. RABBIT: You look upset! What's the matter?

FANNY *(Breathlessly):* We came to warn you.

SCOTT: It's Charles, the White House gardener. He hates rabbits.

FANNY: And he knows you're here with us.

MR. RABBIT: Don't worry. I know how to hide from gardeners. I've had lots of practice!

FANNY: But you are in great danger.

SCOTT: You must leave at once!

MR. RABBIT: How can I leave before Easter? I have too much to do. Now tell me—have you asked your father—I should say, President Hayes—about our surprise?

SCOTT: I meant to ask him last night, but he was so busy—

MR. RABBIT *(Upset):* Here it is almost Easter, and we still don't have permission to have an Easter egg rolling on the White House lawn.

SCOTT: As President of the United States, he has more important things on his mind.

MR. RABBIT: There's *nothing* more important. Don't you understand we're making history?

FANNY: Please don't be angry, Mr. Rabbit. We'll ask him this afternoon. Honest!

MR. RABBIT: You'd better hurry. Right now I have one hundred dozen eggs already in place.

SCOTT: One hundred dozen!

MR. RABBIT: And we'll have twice that many by tomorrow—enough for all the children in Washington.

FANNY *(Excitedly):* The egg rolling will be such fun, all those boys and girls hunting for Easter eggs on our lawn.

SCOTT: We never did anything like that when we lived in Ohio.

MR. RABBIT: There's never been anything like it in Washington, either. If you two do your part, we'll have a "famous first." Now run along. And if you can't find your father, ask your mother.

FANNY *(Shaking her head):* Not this morning, Mr. Rabbit. Mother is too upset about her Easter bonnet.

MR. RABBIT: Doesn't she like it?

SCOTT: It hasn't come yet, and she's afraid it won't arrive in time.

FANNY: And besides, Charles, the gardener, wants to talk to her about you. He says you're ruining the garden.

MR. RABBIT: Nonsense! We Easter rabbits never hurt anybody's garden.

FANNY: Just the same, you'd better watch out for him. He means business.

MR. RABBIT: I'll be careful. Now, please hurry. *(SCOTT and FANNY exit.)* Problems! Problems! Nothing but problems! *(SCOTT runs on.)*

SCOTT: Quick! Quick, Mr. Rabbit! Charles is coming this way! Go hide!

MR. RABBIT: Thanks. I'll go, but I shall return! *(Rushes off left, followed by SCOTT. CHARLES enters right.)*

CHARLES *(Angrily; shaking his head):* If I get my hands on one of those pesky rabbits! I thought I saw one in here just a minute ago. *(Pokes in shrubs with rake, as MARIE and PIERRE enter. PIERRE carries a large hatbox, tied with a ribbon.)*

MARIE: Is it much further, Pierre? I'm tired.

PIERRE: I told you not to come. You always hate to walk in the sun.

MARIE: But I do want to see the White House and Mrs. Hayes. I've never seen a First Lady before.

PIERRE: And you might not see her now. Mamma said we

may leave the hatbox with one of the servants.

MARIE: Let's sit down a minute and rest, Pierre. It's so cool and shady here. And I want to look at the flowers.

PIERRE (*Placing hatbox on bench and mopping his forehead*): All right. But we can't stay too long.

MARIE (*Stooping to pick flower*): Look at this pretty pink flower. I wonder what it is.

CHARLES (*Turning and seeing them*): Here! Here! Here! Keep your fingers off those flowers, young lady!

MARIE: You scared me! Who are you?

CHARLES (*Proudly*): I am the White House gardener. And we can't have children running all over the grounds. Now off with you!

PIERRE: But we're *not* running all over the grounds. We're here on business.

MARIE: Important business. We are from La Belle Bonnet Shoppe, and we have come to deliver the First Lady's Easter bonnet.

CHARLES: Is that so?

PIERRE: Yes, sir. My mother designed it especially for Mrs. Hayes.

CHARLES (*Grumpily*): In that case, I suppose I cannot chase you out. (*Pointing*) The White House is that way. Now I must go tend to my lilies.

MARIE: Please, sir, may we go with you? We haven't see any lilies since we left France.

CHARLES: They are my favorite flower, too. Come along. I'll let you have a peek.

MARIE *and* PIERRE: Oh, thank you, thank you!

CHARLES: But mind you don't touch anything.

MARIE: We won't!

PIERRE: We'll be most careful. (CHARLES, MARIE, *and* PIERRE *exit right, leaving hatbox on bench.* FLOPSY *and* MOPSY *enter left.*)

MOPSY: Did you find out why Mr. Rabbit wants so many eggs this year?

FLOPSY: He hasn't said a word. It must be a state secret.

MOPSY *(Pointing to hatbox):* Look! What is that box?

FLOPSY: Maybe it has something to do with Mr. Rabbit's secret.

MOPSY: Let's look! *(They untie ribbon, remove lid, and lift out a fancy Easter bonnet, covered with flowers.)*

FLOPSY: An Easter bonnet!

MOPSY: I'm going to try it on. *(Does so)*

FLOPSY: It's beautiful! Let me tie the ribbons under your chin. *(Does so)* There!

MOPSY: Let's go show Mr. Rabbit. Maybe he will let me wear it in our Bunny Parade. Take the box. *(FLOPSY and MOPSY exit right with bonnet and hatbox, as MRS. RUTHERFORD B. HAYES, the First Lady, enters left with SCOTT and FANNY.)*

SCOTT: Please, Mother, we have something to ask you.

FANNY: It's very important.

MRS. HAYES: It will have to wait until I have spoken with the gardener. He is bothered about the rabbits on the White House lawn.

FANNY: Oh, Mother, he just doesn't like rabbits.

MRS. HAYES: They can be very harmful to plants and flowers.

SCOTT: Not *these* rabbits. They wouldn't hurt a thing.

MRS. HAYES *(Looking at flower beds):* I must say, the garden looks lovely. I don't see any damage. *(CHARLES enters right with MARIE and PIERRE.)*

PIERRE: The lilies are beautiful, sir. Thank you for showing them to us.

CHARLES: I think they will be perfect by Easter morning. *(Sees MRS. HAYES)* Ah, good morning, ma'am. I'm sorry I was not here to greet you. I was just showing our lilies to these children from La Belle Bonnet Shoppe.

MRS. HAYES: La Belle Bonnet Shoppe? Then you must have brought my Easter bonnet.

PIERRE: Yes, ma'am. It's right here—*(Turns toward bench and sees box is gone)* The hatbox is gone!

MARIE *(In dismay):* But you left it right there—right on that bench!

FANNY: You two must be dreaming.

PIERRE: But I put it there myself! All tied in beautiful ribbons.

MRS. HAYES *(Agitated):* My Easter bonnet! Where could it be?

CHARLES: There was no one else in the garden, ma'am. And we were gone only a few minutes.

PIERRE: Oh, Madame Hayes, how can you ever forgive us? Mamma will be so upset!

MARIE *(Starting to cry):* And it was so beautiful. Mamma worked so hard to make it especially beautiful for you. What shall we do?

MRS. HAYES: There, there! Don't cry, child. It must be here somewhere.

FANNY: Maybe it blew into the bushes.

SCOTT: Impossible. There's hardly any wind.

FANNY: Just the same, we can look, can't we? *(As FANNY and SCOTT start to search bushes, MR. RABBIT enters with hatbox.)*

MR. RABBIT: Excuse me. Is this what you are looking for?

ALL: The hatbox!

FANNY: Oh, Mr. Rabbit, where did you find it!

CHARLES *(Brandishing rake):* There he is, the villain! This time I'll get him! *(Grabs MR. RABBIT by coat collar)*

SCOTT *(Rushing to his rescue):* Let Mr. Rabbit go! Don't hurt him!

FANNY: He is our friend.

MR. RABBIT *(Freeing himself from* CHARLES *and tipping his hat to* MRS. HAYES): With my compliments and best wishes for a happy Easter. *(Hands hatbox to* MRS. HAYES*)*

MRS. HAYES: Thank you! Thank you! *(Opening box and lifting out bonnet)* It *is* lovely. There won't be another one like it in all of Washington. *(To* PIERRE *and* MARIE*)* You may tell your mother I am well pleased.

MARIE *(With a curtsy):* Thank you, ma'am.

PIERRE: Thank you.

MRS. HAYES: As for you, Mr. Rabbit, how can I thank you for finding my beautiful Easter bonnet?

CHARLES: Please, ma'am, this is one of those garden wreckers I was telling you about. He's good for nothing but rabbit stew.

SCOTT: Oh, please, Mother, don't let anyone hurt him.

CHARLES: The White House lawn will be ruined if it is overrun with rabbits.

FANNY: *These* rabbits never hurt anything.

MR. RABBIT *(With dignity):* If I may be allowed to say a word, ma'am. . . .

MRS. HAYES: Please, go ahead.

MR. RABBIT: As you can see, I'm no ordinary rabbit. My card, ma'am. *(With a bow, he hands* MRS. HAYES *a card.)*

MRS. HAYES *(Reading):* "Mr. Easter Rabbit—Colored Eggs a Specialty."

SCOTT: He really is the Easter Rabbit, Mother.

FANNY: And he has one hundred dozen Easter eggs hidden on our lawn.

MRS. HAYES: One hundred dozen!

MR. RABBIT: With more to come, ma'am, as soon as my helpers finish dyeing them.

MRS. HAYES: But how can we possibly use all of those eggs at the White House?

SCOTT: That's what we wanted to ask you about, Mother.

FANNY: Mr. Rabbit has the most wonderful idea.

MR. RABBIT: Perhaps I can explain, ma'am. There are many children in this city who believe in the Easter Rabbit, but they never have the pleasure of hunting for Easter eggs. Now, it is my idea, ma'am, that this big lawn would make an ideal place for an Easter egg rolling. An Easter egg hunt, you might say.

CHARLES: Never! Not on the White House lawn. I won't stand for it.

MRS. HAYES: But the White House belongs to the people of the United States and to their children. *(Turns)* Mr. Rabbit, this is a fine idea. I am sure President Hayes will approve.

SCOTT *and* FANNY *(Hugging her):* Oh, thank you, Mother! Thank you!

MR. RABBIT: Madam, you have won a place for yourself in history. You will always be remembered as the First Lady who started the custom of rolling eggs on the White House lawn on Easter morning!

MARIE: May Pierre and I come too?

MRS. HAYES: Of course, my dears. The White House egg rolling must be for one and all. *(To* MR. RABBIT*)* But are you sure, Mr. Rabbit, that you will have enough eggs?

MR. RABBIT: You may see for yourself, ma'am. The second load is just arriving. *(Blows whistle and rabbits enter again with baskets of Easter eggs)*

RABBITS *(Singing to tune of "Skip to My Lou"):*
> Rabbits at the White House,
> What will they do?
> Rabbits at the White House,
> What will they do?
> Rabbits at the White House,
> What will they do?
> What will they do for Easter?
> They'll dye the Easter eggs
> Red, white and blue,
> They'll dye the Easter eggs,
> Red, white and blue,
> They'll dye the Easter eggs,
> Red, white and blue,
> That's what they'll do for Easter!

MR. RABBIT: Attention, fellow workers! I have an announcement from Mrs. Hayes, First Lady of the land!

MRS. HAYES: Tomorrow, Easter Sunday, we will have an Easter egg rolling on the White House lawn. And every Easter from now on, I hope!

SCOTT: For all the children of Washington, D.C.

RABBITS: Hooray! Hooray! Hooray!

CHARLES: I *still* don't like it!

MRS. HAYES, SCOTT *and* FANNY *(Singing to the tune of "Skip to My Lou"):*
> Rabbits at the White House,

CHARLES: Shoo! Shoo! Shoo!

MRS. HAYES, SCOTT *and* FANNY:
> Rabbits at the White House,

CHARLES: Shoo! Shoo! Shoo!

MRS. HAYES, SCOTT *and* FANNY:
> We'll have a jolly Easter!

ALL:

> We'll roll the Easter eggs,
> That's what we'll do.
> Eggs of red and white and blue,
> We'll roll them on the White House lawn,
> That's what we'll do for Easter!
> *(Curtain)*

THE END

The Magic Carpet Sweeper

LINDA LAWSON
JIMMY LAWSON
KAY LAWSON
JOEY LAWSON
MRS. LAWSON
TONY MARVIN

TIME: *The day before Mother's Day.*
SETTING: *The Lawson living room, which adjoins dining room. Sofa, several chairs, desk, end tables, and lamps make up the furnishings.*
AT RISE: LINDA, JIMMY, *and* KAY *are seated around a table composing a poem.*
LINDA: What will rhyme with mother besides *other* and *brother?* We need just the right word for this Mother's Day poem.
KAY: How about "ruther?"
LINDA *(Puzzled):* Ruther? That's not a word!
KAY: Of course it is. And I already have it in a rhyme. "I'd ruther have you for my mother than any other!"
LINDA *and* JIMMY *(Laughing):* That's a good one, Kay!
LINDA: You're thinking of the word *rather.*
JIMMY: You'd have to say: "I'd rather have you for my mather than any ather!"

170

KAY (*Sighing heavily*): I told you from the beginning we should have bought a Mother's Day card instead of trying to write a poem ourselves.

LINDA: What would we use for money?

JIMMY: It's taken every cent we could scrape together to buy Mom the earrings and bracelet.

KAY: I guess you're right. I hope Mr. Kline saved the bracelet for us.

LINDA: I'm sure he did. When we bought the earrings from him last week, I told him we'd be back for the bracelet if we could possibly get the money.

KAY (*Worried; looking at watch*): I hope Joey gets to the store before it closes. You know how he sometimes gets sidetracked.

JIMMY: Stop worrying, Kay. He'll make it. He knows we're depending on him.

KAY: I guess you're right, Jimmy. (*After a pause*) Let's look at the earrings again.

LINDA (*Rising and going to desk*): We'll wear them out just by looking at them. (*Takes package from drawer*)

JIMMY: Why did you leave them in the desk where Mom might find them?

LINDA: I just brought them down from my room this morning to show them to Rachel Evans when she comes over later on. (*Opens box*) Look! Aren't they beautiful?

JIMMY (*Dismayed*): There's only one! Where's the other one?

LINDA (*Frantically*): It must be here. They were both in the box this morning.

KAY: Are you sure, Linda?

LINDA: Of course! Last night I brought the box down to show the earrings to Daddy. I'm sure they were both in the box when I put it back.

JIMMY *(Upset):* This is terrible! You should have been more careful.

KAY *(Angrily):* Don't blame Linda, Jimmy. I saw you showing the earrings to Danny Martin yesterday after school.

JIMMY: That was before Linda showed them to Dad.

LINDA *(Upset):* Who would have taken one earring?

KAY: Probably nobody. It's just lost.

JIMMY: Well, we'd better start searching the house. *(Starts looking around on floor)*

LINDA: I'll look on the stairs.

KAY: I'll check the bedroom. *(As* LINDA *and* KAY *start to exit,* JOEY *enters. He carries carpet sweeper, clumsily wrapped in brown paper.)*

JOEY: Surprise! Wait till you see what I have!

JIMMY: Did you get the bracelet?

JOEY: No. I saw something Mom really wants.

LINDA *(Agitated):* Joey, what are you talking about? You know perfectly well you were supposed to get that bracelet to go with the earrings!

KAY: That's what we all wanted.

JOEY: Sure, that's what *you* wanted. But I got something Mom wants. *(Holds up package with carpet sweeper)*

JIMMY: What is it? It looks like a giant floor lamp.

KAY: Or a giant umbrella.

JOEY: You're both wrong. *(Removes paper)* It's a carpet sweeper!

OTHERS *(Dumbfounded):* A carpet sweeper!

LINDA: Joey Lawson! How could you do such a thing!

KAY: That's a terrible Mother's Day present! Besides, Mom already has one.

JOEY: This is no ordinary sweeper. It's a *magic* carpet sweeper.

LINDA *(Scornfully):* Magic! Whoever heard of a magic

carpet sweeper? That's ridiculous, Joey!

JOEY: But it is. Look—it says so. *(Points to word "Magic" pasted in gold letters on base of sweeper)*

JIMMY: Joey, that's only the trade name.

JOEY: What's a trade name?

JIMMY: Just a name the manufacturer made up. They could have called it the "Golden Sweeper" or the "Diamond Sweeper." The label doesn't mean it's really magic.

KAY: You take that thing right back.

LINDA: And get a refund.

JOEY: I can't. I bought it at the secondhand store, and there's a big sign that says, "No Returns."

LINDA: Oh, no! What made you do such a crazy thing?

JOEY: 'Cause I know it's what Mom wants. She's always saying she wishes there were some magic way to keep this house clean, so when I saw this "Magic" sweeper in the window, I went in and bought it. It was a real bargain.

KAY: Bargain! Not if we don't want it.

JOEY: Tony Marvin gave me a special price. When I told him I had only ten fifty, he said I could have it for that.

KAY: And you spent our good money for a broken-down, second-hand carpet sweeper.

LINDA: We should never have sent you.

KAY: You're too little.

JOEY *(Indignantly)*: I'm not too little to know that Mom wants something magic to help her with the housework—not some old bracelet. And this is a *real* magic sweeper.

JIMMY: How do you know?

JOEY *(Grabbing handle of sweeper)*: I—I can feel it. When I take hold of this handle, it feels like magic and little tingles run up and down my arm. And when I push it *(Pushes it back and forth)*, the tingles get bigger and bigger. *(Others look at each other and shake heads as* JOEY *pushes sweeper.)*

LINDA: Here . . . let me try. *(Reaches for handle)*

JOEY *(Pushing her away)*: No. You'll spoil it.

LINDA *(Eagerly)*: Come on, Joey. Just let me try.

JOEY: O.K. Only for a little while, though. *(*LINDA *takes handle very gingerly and pushes sweeper around room.)*

JIMMY: Do you feel anything?

LINDA: I—I'm not sure. *(After a few more tries)* Yes, yes. I think I do. *(Sweeps harder)* Now I'm sure of it. *(Pushes sweeper toward others)* Get out of my way, everybody. Let me sweep over there near the table.

JIMMY: Aw, go on. I'll bet you don't feel a thing.

KAY: Give me a turn, Linda.

LINDA: In a minute. Stand back. I want to sweep under the sofa. *(She continues sweeping, as others dart out of the way.)*

KAY: Come on. It's my turn now.

JIMMY: You'll wear out the rug with all this sweeping.

KAY: I'll do the dining room. Mom said this morning there were some crumbs on the floor.

LINDA *(Reluctantly)*: All right, but be careful. I'm beginning to think there really is something magic about this.

KAY: Let me see for myself. *(Takes handle and sweeps back and forth in dining area)*

LINDA: How does it feel?

KAY: I can't say, exactly. It doesn't feel like an ordinary sweeper.

JOEY: The harder you push it, the better it feels.

KAY *(Sweeping more vigorously and heading toward dining room)*: I see what you mean. I'm going to give it a real workout under the dining room table.

JIMMY: I still don't believe it.

LINDA: Just wait till you try it.

JIMMY: Who, me? Can you see me pushing a carpet sweeper?

LINDA: It wouldn't hurt you. You're always trying to get out of working around the house.

KAY (*Moving back into living room area with sweeper; excitedly*): You know, you're right. There *is* something magic about this sweeper. I'm going to take it upstairs and try it in my room.

JIMMY: Do you really mean it, Kay?

KAY: Sure, I mean it. It's definitely different.

JIMMY: O.K. I'll give it a try.

KAY: Not till after I've used it in my room. (*Moves toward door*)

JIMMY: My room's dirtier than yours. Let me try it first.

KAY: I'd better show you how to use it. Boys are so awkward at this sort of thing. Come on. (KAY *and* JIMMY *exit.*)

LINDA (*Sighing*): Joey, you've upset our whole Mother's Day surprise. (*Shakes head*) That carpet sweeper can't really be magic.

JOEY: You said yourself you felt tingles up and down your arm.

LINDA: I know it *felt* like magic. But my common sense tells me it couldn't be true.

JOEY: I'm glad I don't have too much common sense to believe in magic.

LINDA: Anyway, we can't get the bracelet, the way we planned.

JOEY: We still have the earrings.

LINDA: No, we don't. One of them is missing.

JOEY (*Upset*): What happened to it?

LINDA: We don't know. I had the earrings in my bureau drawer, then I put them there in the desk. *(Points)* We've been showing them around so much that somehow or other one of them got lost.

JOEY: That's terrible. *(More cheerfully)* Then you should be glad we have the magic carpet sweeper to give Mom.

LINDA *(Stamping her foot):* Stop calling it a *magic* carpet sweeper. (KAY *and* JIMMY *return with sweeper.)*

JIMMY *(Excitedly):* This sweeper is really something! It tore around my room as if it had a mind of its own. I never had such a good time cleaning my room.

KAY *(Sarcastically):* You never tried cleaning it before!

JOEY: Do you really think it's magic?

JIMMY: I don't know. It feels like magic.

LINDA: Did you feel the tingles?

JIMMY: I sure did.

LINDA: I don't know what to think.

KAY: It doesn't really make much difference what we think. It's the only present we have for Mom.

JIMMY: Right. Then what are we waiting for? Let's get out the fancy paper and ribbon and make it look like a special gift.

LINDA: With all the cleaning we've done, it should be pretty full.

KAY: I'll get a newspaper, and we can empty it. *(Takes newspaper from table and spreads it out on floor)*

JIMMY *(Emptying sweeper):* Wow! We picked up a lot of dirt!

KAY *(Pointing to dirt on paper):* Look! What's that sparkling in the dust?

LINDA: Where? *(Goes nearer to look closely)*

KAY: Right there.

JIMMY *(Picking it up):* It's Mom's earring!

JOEY *(Grinning):* Now maybe you'll believe this sweeper is really magic. It finds lost articles. *(They all bend down to look.)*

JIMMY: I lost a quarter somewhere yesterday. I wonder if that's in here.

KAY: There's the gold button that fell off my dress. *(Pretends to pick up button off floor)* I've looked everywhere for it! *(As they are crouched around paper, MRS. LAWSON enters, wearing coat and carrying some small packages.)*

MRS. LAWSON: What in the world are you children doing?

ALL *(Jumping up, startled; ad lib):* Mom! Where did you come from! *(Etc.)*

LINDA: You weren't supposed to come home for another hour.

MRS. LAWSON: I got an earlier bus. What's wrong? Did I interrupt something?

KAY *(Looking at others; nervously):* Uh—no. It's just that . . .

JIMMY: You walked in right in the middle of our surprise.

MRS. LAWSON: I'm sorry, but it's enough of a surprise to find you with a carpet sweeper. Don't tell me you've been cleaning your rooms!

JOEY *(Blurting it out):* It's your present, Mom. Look . . . a "Magic Carpet Sweeper."

MRS. LAWSON: A carpet sweeper! But darlings, I already have one.

JOEY: I know, Mom, but this is different. It's magic!

LINDA: Mom, it was all Joey's idea. He thinks it's magic because it says "Magic" on the label.

JIMMY: It really does feel different, Mom. I noticed it when I cleaned my room.

MRS. LAWSON *(Amazed):* When you *what*?

JIMMY: When I cleaned my room. It felt sort of tingly.

KAY: And I noticed the same thing when I used it in my room and in the dining room.

MRS. LAWSON *(Looking around at all of them):* You mean you actually cleaned the dining room and your bedrooms?

KAY: Sure.

LINDA: When I did this room, I must admit I felt little tingles up and down my arm.

MRS. LAWSON *(Smiling):* Then there's no question about it. This sweeper really is magic.

JOEY: Do you really think so, Mom?

MRS. LAWSON: I certainly do. Any sweeper that could get you children to clean your rooms without being told is solid gold magic, and no mistake.

JIMMY: It didn't seem like work at all. It seemed more like fun.

KAY: Jimmy and I even fought over taking turns.

MRS. LAWSON: Then it must be real magic. Joey, it's a wonderful present. Where did you find it?

JOEY *(Proudly):* It was in the second-hand store window. A boy in our school who works there sold it to me . . . Tony Marvin. *(Doorbell rings.)*

TONY *(Offstage):* Hey, Joey, may I come in? *(*TONY MARVIN *enters, cap in hand.)*

JOEY: Hi, Tony. What are you doing here? *(Turns)* Mom, this is Tony, the boy who sold me the magic carpet sweeper.

MRS. LAWSON: Hello, Tony.

TONY: Glad to meet you, Mrs. Lawson.

JIMMY: Mom loves her sweeper, Tony.

TONY: That's too bad. I mean . . . that's great, Mrs. Lawson, but, well, my mother sent me over to bring the sweeper back.

KAY *(Indignantly):* But you can't do that. Joey paid you for it.

TONY: Yeah, but you see, the sweeper wasn't for sale. It was just sitting there in the window. Mom had been cleaning up the window carpeting and the phone rang . . . and, well, when she came back I had sold her sweeper. She was pretty cross with me.

MRS. LAWSON: It was a natural mistake, Tony, and *(Laughing)* I think you were a very good salesman.

JOEY *(Sadly):* Then it isn't really magic?

TONY: The carpet sweeper? Magic? Who ever said it was?

JOEY *(Pointing to letters on sweeper):* But the gold letters say "Magic."

TONY: You can't believe everything you read, Joey. Look, I'm sorry. Here's your money. *(Hands bills and coins to JOEY)* I have to get back with this. So long, everybody. *(Picks up sweeper and exits)*

LINDA *(Sighing):* There goes your Mother's Day present!

KAY: And I was beginning to think it really was magic.

JIMMY: It was magic enough to find the missing earring.

LINDA: Yes, Mom, at least we have these for your Mother's Day surprise. *(Gets box, puts in second earring, and hands it to MRS. LAWSON)*

MRS. LAWSON: How beautiful! *(Puts them on)* Just what I wanted.

JOEY: One was lost but the magic carpet sweeper found it.

JIMMY: That sweeper wasn't magic at all, Joey.

LINDA: Only a little boy like you would have been fooled.

JOEY *(Angrily):* I don't care what you say. It was magic. *(Emphatically)* It was, it was!

MRS. LAWSON: Don't be so upset, Joey. I think there really was magic in that carpet sweeper.

JOEY: You do?

MRS. LAWSON: Yes, I do. It turned work into play. Every week, I coax, and plead, and beg, and order, and command until I get you children to do your chores around the house.

ALL *(Ad lib; sheepishly):* I guess you're right, Mom. We know. We'll try harder. *(Etc.)*

MRS. LAWSON: The magic of the sweeper made the work easy because you *wanted* to do it.

LINDA: But what about those mysterious tingles?

MRS. LAWSON: A little imagination is a wonderful tingler, Linda. You'd be surprised how many tingles you'd feel if you'd use our old sweeper more often.

JOEY: You mean there might be magic in that?

MRS. LAWSON: There's magic everywhere, Joey, if you just look for it, and have love enough to know it when you see it.

LINDA: Mom, I think I'm beginning to catch on. *(Runs off for a moment, then re-enters with dustcloth)* How would you like this magic dustcloth for your Mother's Day gift? I promise to use it every day, just to feel those magic tingles.

MRS. LAWSON: Wonderful, Linda! Thank you so much.

KAY: Wait a minute, Mom. I have a magic present for you, too. *(She darts off.)*

JIMMY: I know where there's a piece of magic you could use. *(Exits)*

JOEY: So do I! *(Exits)*

LINDA: I think you'd rather have your magic presents than any bracelet we could buy.

MRS. LAWSON: I'm sure of that, dear.

KAY *(Entering with dish towel):* Here's a magic dish towel. You won't have to tell me to dry the dishes any more. I'll dry them by magic.

JIMMY (*Entering with polishing cloth*): Here's the magic polisher for the car. It will be so shiny, you'll never recognize it.

JOEY (*Entering with bottle of window cleaner and cloth*): If I'm going to clean the windows, this magic potion will help.

JIMMY: From now on you'll get your housework done by magic for sure, won't you, Mom?

MRS. LAWSON: I sure will, Jimmy, and it will be the best magic of all—the magic of love. (*All crowd around and hug* MRS. LAWSON.)

LINDA: Listen, I just thought of the perfect rhyme to go with *Mother*.

ALL (*Ad lib*): What is it? Tell us! (*Etc.*)

LINDA: *Love her!* Now we can finish our Mother's Day poem. (*Recites*) The best gift for Mother

KAY *and* JIMMY: From sister and brother

JOEY: Is show that you love her

ALL: Each day of the year. (*Curtain falls.*)

THE END

Production Notes

THE GREEDY GOBLIN
(Play on pages 3–16)

Characters: 6 male; 3 female.

Playing Time: 25 minutes.

Costumes: Goblin is dressed in solid green. A hooded mask covers his face; the mask should have large phosphorescent eyes painted on it. A long loose duster covers the Goblin from head to heels; he carries a green feather and a note (to leave on the table) in his pocket. Mr. Strudel wears the traditional white baker's cap and apron. All others wear everyday dress. Mr. Whitman has coat and hat.

Properties: Newspaper; pumpkin pie; serving knife; flashlight; tray for paper plates, napkins, forks and cinnamon shaker.

Setting: The Whitman living room, with small stand center, at least four chairs, a telephone, a table with black thread in the drawer, and a desk with paper on it and four flashlights in a drawer. Entrances are right and left.

Lighting: Stage lights out and up, as indicated in text.

THE SOFTHEARTED GHOST
(Play on pages 17–27)

Characters: 5 male; 3 female; male and female extras for Masqueraders and Stagehands.

Playing Time: 25 minutes.

Costumes: Mother, Father, and Egbert are dressed in long, white robes or sheets, with clanging chains around their waists as belts. Gypsy wears appropriate costume. Pierrette wears a black and white clown costume. M.C. wears long-tailed coat, high silk hat, and pair of gym shorts. Mr. Static is dressed in everyday clothes. Girls wear various Halloween costumes.

Properties: Magazine, compact with mirror, microphone.

Setting: Scene 1: A modern living room (more macabre decorations may be added). Scene 2: Piano with bench; folding chair; microphone on stand.

Lighting: Spotlight in Scene 2; lights black out, as indicated in text.

Sound: "The Funeral March" or other melancholy music; recording may be used.

THE RUNAWAY UNICORN
(Play on pages 28–38)

Characters: 18 male; 5 female.

Playing Time: 20 minutes.

Costumes: Traditional storybook costumes. Linda and Lewis wear school clothes. The Unicorn Keeper wears a uniform. The Unicorn wears a Unicorn costume, with a white body, a horse's head, and a single horn, which is black in the middle and red at the tip.

Properties: Horn; book; crown.

Setting: Storybook Lane in Bookland. Onstage are large cardboard posters represent-

183

ing nine books: ROBIN HOOD, ALICE IN WONDERLAND, PINOCCHIO, PETER RABBIT, MOTHER GOOSE, HANSEL AND GRETEL, SNOW WHITE, JACK AND THE BEANSTALK, and THE WIZARD OF OZ. Backdrop shows Mother Hubbard's house.
Lighting: No special effects.

THANKS TO BUTTER-FINGERS
(Play on pages 39–53)

Characters: 2 male; 3 female.
Playing Time: 20 minutes.
Costumes: Modern, everyday dress. Charlotte has blond wig; Betsy, dark pigtails. Dean wears glasses. Mrs. Upton and Dr. Rinehart wear coats near end.
Properties: Centerpiece of fruit and autumn leaves; stack of plates; trays with glasses and silver; dustpan; broom; long piece of plywood; extension cord; large jar of cold cream; ring; dish towel; sugar bowl.
Setting: The Upton dining room. At center is large table covered with a cloth. Chairs are placed around it. Small side table is nearby; electric coffeepot is set on it. China closet is against the upstage wall.
Lighting: No special effects.

PILGRIM PARTING
(Play on pages 54–66)

Characters: 9 male; 5 female; male and female extras.
Playing Time: 20 minutes.
Costumes: All wear typical Pilgrim dress except Sailor Humphrey and Master Jones, who are dressed for sailing.
Properties: Small sea chest, two cloaks, covered basket, parcel, letter.
Setting: A beach. There may be some boxes and trunks to one side and perhaps some driftwood. Otherwise the stage is bare. If possible, there should be a backdrop representing the sea and sky.
Lighting: No special effects.

SQUEAKNIBBLE'S CHRISTMAS
(Play on pages 67–74)

Characters: 2 male; 3 female; 5 male or female.
Playing Time: 10 minutes.
Costumes: Mr. Grandfather Clock wears a large clock face and a long white beard. The mice wear gray or brown costumes with perky round ears and long, thin tails. Master Puss wears a furry costume with a long tail, pointed ears, and long whiskers. He has sharp claws on his paws. He adds fur coat and cap later in play.
Properties: Gong and hammer.
Setting: The Great Hall of a large house. Mr. Grandfather Clock, holding gong, stands in one corner. On a low table against wall there is a small Christmas tree. Chairs stand at either side of table. Large hammer rests on chair near Mr. Clock. A large sign over center entrance reads MOUSEHOLE.
Lighting: A spotlight is used to

set off the parts of the play in which Squeaknibble appears.

THE CHRISTMAS UMBRELLA
(Play on pages 75–87)

Characters: 6 male; 7 female; 10 male or female for Tinsel, Jingle, and Neighbors.
Playing Time: 20 minutes.
Costumes: Tinsel and Jingle, green and red elf costumes. Santa and Mrs. Santa, traditional costumes. Mrs. Santa wears glasses. Mama, Papa, and Grandma, modern, everyday dress. Umberto children, pajamas and bathrobes. Neighbors, coats and hats.
Properties: Crossword puzzle; pencil; large box; teapot; cup and saucer; plate of cookies; two signs with INVISIBLE printed on them, in tinsel; large box containing nine umbrellas; Christmas tree lights, balls, tinsel; umbrella stripped of covering; stand for umbrella; small radio.
Setting: Scene 1: Santa's Workshop, with door at right. Upstage wall is lined with empty shelves. Workbenches are left and right. Up center are small table and rocking chair. Fireplace is in back wall. Scene 2: Umberto living room, plainly furnished with couch and a few easy chairs. Exits are right and left. Up center is large table.
Lighting: No special effects.
Sound: Knocking; recorded music to "Deck the Halls."

SOFTY THE SNOWMAN
(Play on pages 88–98)

Characters: 2 male; 4 female; 6 male or female for Toy Buyers and Spunky; as many male and female extras as desired for Santa's Workers.
Playing Time: 15 minutes.
Costumes: Santa wears traditional costume. Toy Buyers wear business suits. Snowman wears battered silk hat, white padded costume, and carries broom. Spunky, Mrs. Santa, and Santa's Workers wear red and green costumes. Mrs. Santa has paper hat, buttons, and pins in apron pocket. Girls wear everyday clothes.
Properties: Mechanical toy, bell, record book, white teddy bear, 3 lists.
Setting: A display room. Santa's desk is up center. On the desk is a bell; large book is in drawer. Shelves of toys, signs and Christmas decorations may be added.
Lighting: No special effects.

A FEBRUARY FAILURE
(Play on pages 99–106)

Characters: 1 male; 2 female; as many male and female extras as desired for Announcer and Students.
Playing Time: 15 minutes.
Costumes: Modern, everyday dress.
Properties: Paper, pencil, picture of Lincoln, package containing framed poster of "Lincoln's Failures."
Setting: Classroom, with large

desk for teacher up center. There are additional desks and chairs for students. Entrance is left. Room may be decorated with appropriate Lincoln posters and pictures.
Lighting: No special effects.

THE MISSING LINC
(Play on pages 107–120)

Characters: 4 male; 3 female.
Playing Time: 20 minutes.
Costumes: Modern everyday clothes. Martha wears a hat and coat.
Properties: Book; glasses; old bill; suitbox, containing boy's suit; package containing manuscript; envelope with letter; purse.
Setting: Living room with comfortable furniture. There is a sofa at one side of stage, with chairs and tables with lamps placed about the room. Exits are right and left.
Lighting: No special effects.
Sound: Doorbell.

THE TREE OF HEARTS
(Play on pages 121–134)

Characters: 5 male; 3 female; as many male and female extras as desired for Children.
Playing Time: 20 minutes.
Costumes: King, Prince, and Chancellor wear appropriate court clothes. Mr. and Mrs. Gooseberry and Goldie wear peasant clothing. Dale and Gail wear everyday, modern dress. Children of Valentia wear peasant skirts, shorts, etc.
Properties: Scroll and quill;

spade; market basket; large straw hat; guidebook; green tub; red paper hearts with wire hangers attached.
Setting: Palace Garden of Valentia, near the Head Gardener's hut. Painted backdrop of flower beds and Mr. Gooseberry's trees may be used. In Scene 2, a folding screen with sign reading HAPPY BIRTHDAY, YOUR HIGHNESS! is center. Small, bare tree stands behind it.
Lighting: No special effects.
Sound: Recording of trumpets.

THE BIRTHDAY PIE
(Play on pages 135–143)

Characters: 6 male; 6 female.
Playing Time: 15 minutes.
Costumes: Appropriate modern dress. Coats for guests.
Properties: Birthday cake decorated with white frosting and red cherries; tray with plates of ice cream; wrapped presents; radio.
Setting: Smith living room. Couch, chairs, tables make up the furnishings. At center are large table and ten chairs; red, white, and blue napkins are placed at place settings, with small placecards. Centerpiece is a hatchet with American flags.
Lighting: No special effects.
Sound: Doorbell.

THE MOUNT VERNON CRICKET
(Play on pages 144–157)

Characters: 5 male; 5 female.
Playing Time: 25 minutes.

Costumes: Modern, everyday dress. All wear outdoor clothing when they first enter. Mr. Harvey has a briefcase containing papers.

Properties: Old-fashioned wooden footstool, two large ugly vases, tray with coffee cups, spoons, etc.

Setting: The living room of the Bailey home. A sofa is at center, with a coffee table in front of it. Armchairs, tables, and a telephone complete the furnishings. Exit at left leads to front door, and exit at right leads to rest of house.

Lighting: No special effects.

Sound: Doorbell, telephone, as indicated in text.

THE WHITE HOUSE RABBIT
(Play on pages 158–169)

Characters: 8 male; 5 female.

Playing Time: 20 minutes.

Costumes: Mr. Rabbit wears a red, white and blue waistcoat, white tights or trousers, silk hat, large watch and chain across a red vest, and a whistle on a cord around his neck. Other rabbits have large "cottontails" and long ears sticking up through hats; they may wear jackets and trousers or skirts. Fanny, Scott and Mrs. Hayes wear clothes of the period. Charles wears overalls,

dark work shirt and old straw hat. Pierre and Marie wear hats and coats.

Properties: Notebook; pencil; baskets filled with Easter eggs (plastic eggs may be used); rake; hatbox; flowers; flowered hat; card.

Setting: Corner of the White House lawn. High shrubs are along the back and side of the stage. Bench is right. Sign with an arrow pointing left reads: TO THE WHITE HOUSE. Several flower beds are visible (may be cut from cardboard).

Sound and Lighting: No special effects.

THE MAGIC CARPET SWEEPER
(Play on pages 170–181)

Characters: 3 male; 3 female.

Playing Time: 20 minutes.

Costumes: Everyday clothes. Mrs. Lawson wears coat.

Properties: Paper and pencil; small box containing earrings; carpet sweeper wrapped in brown paper; gold button; dustcloth; dish towel, polishing cloth; window cleaner; small packages.

Setting: A comfortable living room with sofa, several chairs, desk, end tables, lamps, etc. Newspaper is on table.

Lighting: No special effects.